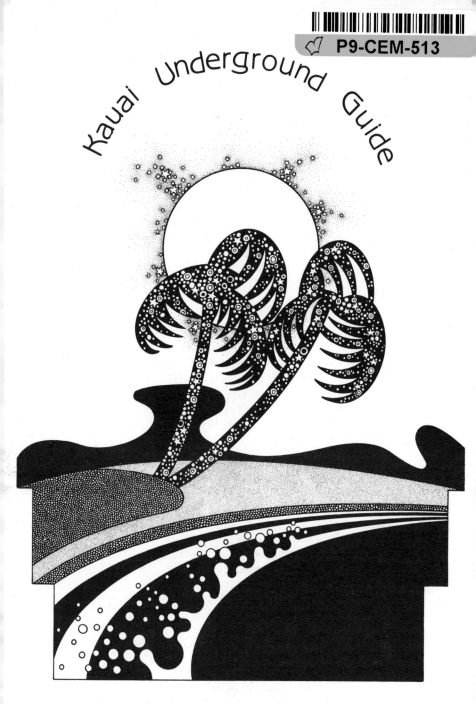

Kauai Underground Guide

Lenore W. Horowitz

P9-CEM-513

**Special thanks to Mirah, Jeremy, Michael, Lauren
and Larry Horowitz
for helping with the research, writing,
illustrating, and layout design of this
tenth anniversary edition.**

©1989 by Papaloa Press, A Division of LCH Enterprises Inc.
All rights reserved
under International and Pan-American
copyright conventions.

ISBN 0-9615498-3-1
ISSN 0886-3482
Library of Congress Catalog card 82-643643

Technical Assistance by Kate Meyer Design, Palo Alto, CA
Color separations by Color Tech, Redwood City, CA
Printed in U.S.A. by Spilman Printing, Sacramento, CA

Contents

Beach Adventures

Restaurants

Exploring Kauai

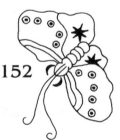

Preface – Magic Kauai

Ten years ago, when we wrote our first edition, Kauai was the undiscovered Hawaiian island. Resorts were relatively small-scale and low-rise, for development was strictly controlled, and buildings could be "no higher than a coconut tree." A tourist could walk for miles on spectacular beaches and encounter only another person or two. Two of the island's three traffic lights were in the main town of Lihue, and the third was at a sugar cane road intersection near Koloa, a sleepy town where the Salvation Army building had the freshest coat of paint. Most of the island was inaccessible, and the main road stopped at either side of the island's northwest quadrant — the spectacular Na Pali wilderness reachable only by boat, helicopter, or narrow and dangerous hiking paths.

Ten years later, most of this is still true, though by now more than a million visitors have discovered Kauai! Tourism has grown to nearly three-fourths of the island's economy, and the number of hotel rooms will soon reach 7,000. A dozen traffic lights are needed to control traffic, and in spite of a new by-pass road, Kauai can still have mainland-style bumper to bumper traffic jams along the main two-lane road at rush hour.

You can still find the magic Kauai, though, if you make the effort to look. So far, development has affected only 4 % of the island, primarily in the south near Poipu and in the east near Lihue, with the rest of the island zoned for conservation or agriculture. Once you drive north of Kapa'a, or west of Hanapepe, you turn the clock back ten years. Mile after mile of pastureland and cane fields stretch to the sea, for the rainfall in the north and the barrenness of the west have so far provided natural barriers to development. While you will find much more to do and eat and see than we did in 1980, you can still find beautiful places to be alone.

This is the Kauai we will try to describe to you in our *Guide*— not what you would see from a tour bus, but the rare and special place we have discovered over the years as tourists and home-owners. We want to share with you our favorite adventures—at the beaches, in restaurants, and on shopping expeditions. We do not describe every restaurant and shop, only those we have visited, and our opinions are shaped by personal preference. We look for peace and quiet, privacy and natural beauty.

In many ways our *Guide* is unique. As a family with four children, we can offer advice on beaches and activities based on having taken babies to Kauai for more than a dozen years! For adults with that enviable freedom to go off by themselves, we describe in detail what one can expect to find in many island restaurants. Even a single year brings dramatic change to this island, and our working vacations keep us busy tracking what's new, what's different, and what's still as lovely as ever. You may find that in some cases prices, menus, even managements may be changed; we'll catch up with them in our next edition! It's been great fun hearing from people all over the country who have enjoyed discovering Kauai with our *Guide,* and who want to help update the next one.

So as we celebrate our tenth anniversary, we want to thank all the readers who have helped make our *Guide* a storybook success. Who would have thought that our first edition of sixteen pages would grow into a book which has sold 50,000 copies! Or that our oldest child Mirah, as a gregarious six-year-old, would arrange such a spectacular send-off by handing our first edition to a friend she made on the beach. He turned out to be Chandler Forman of the *Chicago Sun-Times*, and when his story about Kauai—and our book—was syndicated nationwide, more than 700 letters arrived at our door, and we had to rush to press with a new edition!

Our family has changed over the years, too. We no longer have to search for shade when we go to the beach because our babies are growing up! And, as we share their newest adventures, we see this wonderful island unfold in fascinating new possibilities.

To see Kauai through the eyes of children is to be alive to the magic of rainbows and sandcrabs, to catch fish and give them names, to invent stories about the mountains. Like an old friend, Kauai gets better with each visit. New adventures take us to new places, and at the same time we rediscover with deeper affection what we have loved in the past. We hope you will feel the same way about this special place and return again soon!

Beach Adventures

Map labels (clockwise from top): Haena, Tunnels, Lumahai, Hanalei, Anini, Kalihiwai, Secret Beach, Kilauea Bay, Larson's Beach, Moloa'a, Ke'e Beach, Polihale Beach, Anahola, 56, Barking Sands, Donkey Beach, Kealia, Kokee State Park, Kapaa, Waimea, Infinity Beach, Lydgate, Kekaha, Hanamaulu, Hanapepe, Lihue, 50, Kalapaki Bay, Nawiliwili, Salt Pond Beach, Mahaulepu Beach, Poipu Beach, Shipwreck Beach

Western Shore

Polihale Beach, 11
Barking Sands, 12
Kekaha Beaches, 12
Infinity Beach, 13
Waimea Black Sand Beach, 14
Salt Pond Beach Park, 14

Eastern Shore

Kalapaki Beach, 10
Hanama'ulu Beach, 21
Lydgate Beach Park, 22
Kapa'a Beaches, 24
Kealia Beach, 24
Donkey Beach, 24
Anahola Bay, 25

South Shore

Poipu Beach Park, 16
Brennecke's Beach, 17
Shipwreck Beach, 18
Mahaulepu Beach, 18

North Shore

Moloa'a Bay, 27
Larsen's Beach, 28
Kilauea Bay, 30
Secret Beach, 31
Kalihiwai Bay, 33
Sunset Beach, 34
Anini Beach, 34
Hanalei Bay, 35
Lumahai Beach, 36
Tunnels Beach, 37
Haena Beach Park, 37
Ke'e Beach, 38

8

Touring Kauai

Kauai is like an America in miniature, with rolling hills and valleys to the east and majestic mountains to the west. On the eastern shore, sand as fine as sugar rings half-moon bays fringed with stately ironwood trees. These are the best beaches for walking and hunting for shells and driftwood. On the south shore, the island's flat, leeward side offers protected swimming almost all year round under sunny skies and gentle breezes. We love the north shore, where magnificent cliffs reach to touch the sky, and the foaming, churning surf crashes against the rocks. Here, rain showers freshen the air, dance among the flowers, and make the coastline sparkle. Or go west to Polihale Beach, where you'll find cliffs like the exotic towers of some lost civilization, and golden sand stretching as far as the eye can see. Kauai will never bore you, because a half–hour drive, at the most, can take you to a beach that almost seems to belong to another island.

Different as they are, the beaches also change their moods with the seasons. On the north shore, the sea may be so calm and clear in summer that bubbles on the surface cast shadows on the sandy bottom. But winter tides can turn a peaceful lagoon to a roaring, raging caldron; and ocean spray can drape the valleys with salty mist. In winter, some northern beaches disappear entirely under crashing surf, and boats which anchor peacefully in Hanalei Bay for half the year take shelter in Nawiliwili to the south.

Even the sunsets change with the changing angle of the sun. In winter months, when the sun rides lower in the sky, you'll see the sunset in burnished clouds over the mountains, while in summer, the slender line between sea and sky catches fire in a torrent of gold.

Almost circular in shape, Kauai has three main tourist areas. If you plan carefully, even a three-day escape can have a little of everything. Getting around the island requires only a rental car and some planning. With a shape like a clock face, Kauai is nearly encircled by a main two-lane highway, except for the wilderness area in the northwest quadrant. The main road is easily traveled, so you can get from Lihue to Kapa'a in about 20 minutes, from Kapa'a to Hanalei in about 45 minutes, or from Lihue to Poipu in about 20 minutes, and from Poipu to Polihale in about 35 minutes.

Pack a picnic lunch and some beach mats, and explore the island's most beautiful hidden beaches! In our book, we have arranged the beach descriptions to follow the route you would travel if you were driving counterclockwise around the island, beginning at Polihale Beach at the westernmost end of passable road, and then driving east to Poipu and Lihue and then north to Hanalei until you reach Ke'e Beach at the north-westernmost end of paved road in Ha'ena.

We don't recommend that you follow that route! Instead, read about the beaches and plan your destinations according to the weather and the season. In winter, the surf is more unpredictable and dangerous on the northern and north-eastern beaches, while the best and safest swimming is on the south shore. In summer, the surf is up on the south, and north shore beaches can be beautiful and great for swimming. Whenever you head for the beach, however, follow this simple rule for swimming safety: don't swim alone or too far out at any beach whose currents are unfamiliar to you. Be sure to read 'Beach Safety' (page 40) carefully.

No matter the season, try to explore as much of this wonderful island as you can, especially the north shore where the beaches are by far the most spectacular. They're not as much fun in the rain, however, so plan your travels with an eye to the weather. On a clear day, drive north, because if your visit to Kauai is only a few days, you may not get another chance! If you see rain out your window, on the other hand, drive south or west, where the weather is usually drier. On a really rainy day, unless the storm is island-wide, Polihale might be your best—even your only—dry option! When in doubt, call the weather at 245-3564.

West Coast
Beach Adventures

Polihale Beach

From the time you leave paved road behind to jolt north through a maze of sugar cane fields, you know you're in for something extraordinary. Gradually, beyond the tall sugar cane rustling in the breeze, a dark ridge of jagged peaks appears on the right. As you get closer, these giant cliffs reveal splendid colors— trees and bush in vivid greens against the black rock slashed with the deep red of the volcanic soil. When you can drive no further, the beach at Polihale emerges from the base of the cliffs—an enormous stretch of brilliant white sand more immense, it seems, than the cliffs which tower above and the band of deep blue sea beyond. Only the sky seems the equal of this vast expanse of glaring sand, so wide that to walk from your car to the ocean on a sunny day will burn your feet, and so long that no single vantage point allows the eye to see its full extent. "Beautiful" is too small a word for this awesome place. Polihale—home of spirits—is more appropriate, not only because the majestic cliffs and beach dwarf anything human to insignificance, but also because here man's access to the north coast really ends. Beyond lies the Na Pali wilderness, unreachable except by boat or helicopter, or by the handful of hikers who dare to climb the narrow and dangerous trails. Polihale is the threshold between the known and the unknown, the tamed and the untamed, the familiar and the wild.

The swimming here is treacherous; the rolling, pounding surf even at its most gentle is only for strong, experienced swimmers.

No reefs offer protection from the powerful ocean currents. Come instead for the spectacle, to picnic and walk, to gaze at the grandeur of the cliffs above the endless sea and sand, to listen to the silence broken only by the crashing surf, to appreciate in solitude the splendor of nature's power. A feeling of awe lingers even after you return to paved road and a world of smaller proportions.

Directions: Just before Rt 50 ends, a State Park sign will mark the left turn onto the dirt cane road. Follow signs for about 5 miles to the parking area.

Barking Sands

The beach just south of Barking Sands Missile Range is occasionally available for public use. Call 335-4111 in advance to be sure that the area has not been closed for maneuvers! After signing in at the main gate, you can drive to a long stretch of sandy beach along Major's Bay. Like Polihale Beach, the surf here can be extremely strong, often too powerful for safe swimming, particularly in winter. While the waves break magnificently in long, shining tunnels that look like a surfer's dream, there are unpredictable currents as well as a sudden drop-off just beyond the coral reef which extends almost the full length of the beach. You have to look carefully for channels through the reef to find sandy bottom, or you can go to the northernmost point of the bay where the reef ends. The wide, sandy beach is both hot and difficult to walk on, and shade is almost nonexistent. It is a spectacular place for a picnic, though, and you can see Ni'ihau, purple on the horizon, just past the golden, shining sand and glistening turquoise sea.

Kekaha Beaches

Stretching for miles along Kauai's western coast, the Kekaha beaches combine swimming, surfing, and walking with the predominantly dry weather of the island's leeward side. As Rt 50 curves toward the sea at the small town of Kekaha, the beach is narrow, but a mile or two north, it widens and becomes more golden, with long, rolling waves breaking evenly in brilliant white crests, perfect for surf boards and boogie boards, although in winter months, the surf and currents can be dangerous and unpredictable. At several places along the road, stands of trees provide shade for babies. We recommend driving the full length of this stretch of beaches so that you can select the most favorable spot (ours is across from the swimming pool building) and then double back to park. Despite its clear, sunny weather, the western side of the island has not yet been developed as a tourist area, and so these beaches are frequented primarily by local residents and are not very crowded. The road north of the town towards Barking Sands and Polihale Beach winds through sugar cane fields waving silvery green in the breezes against the deep red-gold of cleared fields and the vivid blues of the sea and the enormous sky.

Infinity Beach

On this lovely, curving beach, the sand and sea are deep gold, as if sprinkled with cinnamon, because of a stream carrying rich red sugar cane soil to the sea. As you walk from the road across a privately owned pasture, you can hear the crash of the waves before you can see the beach, and by the time you pass through the trees which ring the sand, you'll feel you're on a desert island with no people in sight. It is a lovely spot. The waves rise gracefully in long, even lines crested with gold. Each wave breaks and rushes onto the sand in shining foam, and then it rolls back out again to meet the wave coming in. In a fascinating ballet, the waves sometimes meet like dancers in perfect rhythm, and shining spray bursts into the air as they join. Sometimes the waves clash or collide, but there's a beauty even in this more dissonant rhythm. Although you could watch the waves for hours, you would never see two waves embrace in exactly the same way.

The bay is divided by a rocky point reaching well into the water, a spot where local people fish for pompano. To the left is a swimming area protected by a reef, but to reach it you must climb the rocky ledge and cross the rocks, a difficult job in bare feet. To the right of the rocks, the sand stretches a long way before disappearing around a bend. The waves crashing against the sand bring hundreds of shells to the shore. Because Hurricane 'Iwa struck with fury here, many of the trees which ring the beach are still bent and broken, and in the pasture, shattered limbs have been covered by vines and grasses to make extraordinary shapes. There are no facilities, and so small children would not enjoy it, but it's a great place for their parents to escape to for a few hours of peaceful beachcombing and wave-watching.

Directions: Drive north on Rt 50 to the mile 21 marker. Look for a low concrete bridge and a level sandy area on the shoulder of the road for parking. Just north of the bridge, a path leads to a short right-of-way through the pasture to the beach. About 1 mile north on Rt 50 are public restrooms, and a bit further, just across the Waimea River, you'll find some public showers.

Waimea Black Sand Beach

Just off the main street of Waimea town is a long beach, and unusual on Kauai, this one is black sand. The beach looks eerie, as if dusted with coal, and the water is dusky. A recreational fishing pier extends out into the ocean. In this quiet spot, you can wander along the beach and invent stories — perhaps an angry goddess, jealous of the sun mirrored so brightly on the surface of the sea, tried to darken the water and sand with ash from her volcano.

Directions: Between the mile 22 and 23 markers on Rt 50 in the town of Waimea, turn towards the ocean until you find Lau Road. Follow to the end.

Salt Pond Beach Park

What is most astonishing about Salt Pond Beach Park is the intensity of the colors—the brilliant blues of the water and sky, the bright gold of the sand, the vivid greens of sugar cane fields extending in squares and rectangles up the slopes of nearby mountains—all bathed in sunshine that makes everything sparkle. The beach is a perfect semi-circle, where the sand slopes downward with the lovely grace of a golden bowl to hold the sea. A reef near the mouth of this sheltered cove breaks the surf into slow, rolling swells that break again gently near the shore so that children can raft and swim safely most of the year. Rock formations at both ends of the beach create large pools which are calm enough at low tide for babies and toddlers. Older children can try their luck at catching the tiny, swift fish with nets. Walk along the beach and explore tidal pools and the ancient salt ponds where local people still harvest sea salt. The park is spectacular, especially when brightly colored windsurfers race out across the reef, and particularly favored in terms of weather. Even when clouds and rain prevail elsewhere, this little point of land seems to escape them, and in winter, the water seems a few degrees warmer and more friendly.

Showers, rest rooms, picnic tables, and barbecues make this a popular spot for local families and increasingly for tourists, particularly on weekends, although the beach never seems crowded. Pack a picnic lunch or drive about 5 minutes to the Green Garden Restaurant for an inexpensive meal and a slice of fabulous coconut cream or lilikoi chiffon pies.

Directions: Turn onto Rt 543 at Hanapepe, take the first right onto Lokokai Rd, and drive until you see the parking area.

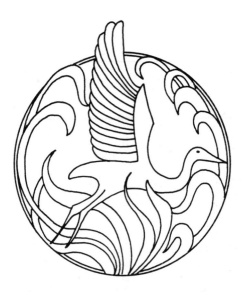

South Shore Beach Adventures

Poipu Beach Park

You could not imagine a more perfect beach for children than this lovely curve of soft golden sand sloping down to a gentle, friendly sea. The waves,with changing shades of turquoise sparkling with sunlight and dazzling white foam, break gently over a protective reef across the entrance to this small cove. For babies and toddlers, a ring of black lava rocks creates a sheltered pool where the water is shallow and still. For older children, waves beyond the pool roll to shore in graceful swells perfect for rafting, under the watchful eye of a county lifeguard. Children also love to explore the long rocky point at the far end of the beach and look for tiny fish trapped in the tidal pools. Bring nets and pails for the hunt! Restrooms, outdoor showers, barbecues, and picnic tables are available. Pavilions offer shade for babies, and swings, a slide and a giant climbing gym will keep older children busy when they tire of the water. "Mama's Beach," as it is called by many local people, is perfect for families, and a great place for a sunset picnic, barbecue, or occasionally, on weekend afternoons, listening to a free concert.

Beyond the rocky point you can explore three crescent shaped, lovely sandy beaches. Just across the point in another sheltered cove is some of the best snorkeling on the island. Hundreds of fish in rainbow colors feed on the coral, so tame they almost swim into your hands. Carry some stale bread or crackers in a plastic bag, and they'll come right to you! Further west, the two beaches in front of the Kiahuna Plantation, the Poipu Beach Hotel, and the Sheraton have stronger surf, terrific for riding and swimming. As you walk along this lovely string of beaches, it is hard to imagine that, the morning after Hurricane 'Iwa, this shoreline was completely straightened and all the sandy spits had washed away.

Since we began coming to Poipu years ago, the number of hotel rooms and apartments sharing these beaches has quadrupled. The effects of recent development are most evident at Poipu Beach Park, long a favorite of both tourists and local residents. The beach gets crowded earlier, stays crowded longer, and is much *more* crowded. Somehow, however, there always seems to be room for one more six-year-old! Come early in the morning or late afternoon, if possible.

Directions: After you pass through Koloa, bear left at the fork near the Kukuiula Stores to the Poipu Beach Road. Pass the Waiohai, turn right on Ho'owili Road then left at Ho'one Road and park in the lot next to Brennecke's, which serves good quality take-out sandwiches. To park at the other beaches, turn left off the Beach Road into the entrance of any of the hotels.

Brennecke's Beach

Legendary for years as the best beach for body surfing, Brennecke's Beach is making a slow reappearance after being completely washed away during Hurricane 'Iwa. The giant boulders hurled into the water by the winds are almost gone now, and the sand is building up the beach slowly. Most important, the currents which created those wonderful long rolling waves are coming back. But not in quite the same pattern. You have to be careful, for today the big rollers break much closer to shore and can throw your boogie board against the rocky sea wall if you are not careful! And every so often, a huge wave comes up, poises with glistening power and then breaks straight down. So if you see the other swimmers dive under a big wave, follow their example!

Directions: Brennecke's is adjacent to Poipu Beach Park on Ho'one Road as you drive east.

Shipwreck Beach

Shipwreck Beach along Ke'oniloa Bay was never much of a beach—until Hurricane 'Iwa blasted the south shore of Kauai and created a new coastline. What was once a thin curve of sand is now enormous, a long, golden crescent divided by lava rocks. To the right of the rocks, the waves roll across a long, shallow reef ending in a rocky point. To the left, the wide, gleaming sand stretches to the base of a low cliff flanked by sand dunes.

This place is called Shipwreck Beach with good reason. The surf is powerful, breaking in long, shining arcs which crest slowly, one at a time, with deceptive smoothness, and then crash in thunderous explosions of spray. Local people warn that beyond the break point are dangerous currents and large rocks. A better place for surfing would be Wailua Beach, where there are life-guards, and rocks are not a problem.

Although Shipwreck Beach is not safe for swimming, the wide sand is great for exercising or running, particularly near the water-line. Climb the cliff to explore strange caves and rock formations. The colors are breathtaking—the deep blue of the water and the gold of the cliffs dazzle the eye, and the view down is a dizzying spectacle of surf crashing against the rocks. Be careful, though. Avoid going close to the cliff's edge, as the footing is slippery with loose sand.

This is a hot place. Bring your own drinks and if you are looking for shade, bring an umbrella. The few scraggly ironwoods which 'Iwa left standing are not much protection from the blistering sun. It's great for photographers but not for children.

Directions: To park at the beach, take Poipu Road. Pass the end of the pavement and go onto the dirt cane road. Turn toward the water at the first opportunity. Construction of the new Hyatt Regency has created a beach access detour. Follow the signs.

Mahaulepu Beach

At the end of a dusty drive through winding sugar cane roads, you will find a beautiful sandy beach carved into a rocky point. This part of the south shore is very dry and very hot — and you'll soon find a thin red film on every surface inside your car, including you!

But it's worth the dust to reach a beach astonishing in its wild beauty, the surf crashing against the rocks and sand, the churning turquoise water almost glowing with sunlight. Beautiful it is, but not for swimming. Except for times when surf on the whole south shore is unusually flat, you'll find the waves crashing with enough force to knock you down, and currents powerful enough to make even local people wary.

Mahaulepu is a lovely beach for exploring. On the eastern end, a lovely half-moon of golden sand nestles at the base of a rocky cliff. A long walk takes you around to the west, past a rocky reef which at low tide juts out of the sand in fascinating formations. As you reach the end of the curve, the tip turns out to be a point, and on the other side, you'll find another, even longer stretch of beach. Here the water ripples in toward shore, protected by an offshore reef where the waves roll in long, even swells. You might see a fisherman casting his line or even a swimmer snorkeling among the rocks where the water is shallow enough to stand. If you continue to the very end, you will find a tidal pool with water shallow and still enough for children. A sandy road winds behind the full length of this beach, and so you can pick almost any spot to park your car. Bring plenty to drink, and perhaps a picnic lunch to eat in the shade of the trees and pretend you are all alone in the world.

Directions: Take the cane road at the end of Poipu Road. Pass the turnoff to Shipwreck Beach and follow the cane road east, passing all narrow dirt roads until you see one that looks wide and well-travelled. Take a right turn onto this road and proceed east until you pass a quarry on the right. At the next intersection, turn right and head toward the water. When you reach the end, you can turn right or left and go to either the east or west end of the beach. The drive covers about 2.5 miles and should take about a quarter hour.

Eastern Shore
Beach Adventures

Kalapaki Beach

Kalapaki Bay is unforgettably beautiful. Almost encircled by mountains on two sides, this natural harbor has a wide sugar sand beach with some of the best swimming on the island. The waves roll to shore in long, even swells and break in shining white crests which are usually great for swimming and rafting. If the surf is too rough, you can stretch out on the warm, golden sand and watch brilliant red and yellow windsurfers or catamarans skim gracefully across the blue water. The horizon is fascinating. On one side, the green ridges of the mountains have the contours of a giant animal sleeping in the sun, while on the other side, houses on stilts perch so precariously on the side of a sheer cliff that you wonder what combination of faith and hope keeps them standing.

The hotel on this beach is the extraordinary Westin Kauai, which is part art museum, part tropical zoo, and part marine aquarium. Some might add, part movie set for Ben Hur filming on Gilligan's Island, for about this very controversial hotel, few people are neutral. Some people love it; others consider it completely out of place on Kauai. You'll have to make up your own mind. But here you'll find Kauai's largest swimming pool, its tallest highrise, its largest collection of south seas art, and its only two-story escalator. You'll also find guests traveling not in cars but in carriages drawn by Clydesdale horses, or in Venetian gondolas on man-made lagoons. Whether you like extravagance on such a spectacular scale, the beach is lovely and, like all beaches on Kauai, is public land. Kalapaki Beach is a favorite spot with our family for boogie boarding when the surf is relatively quiet. Be sure to heed any high surf warnings, however, for at certain times, the waves can break straight down with enormous force, and every so often a really big wave seems to come up out of nowhere to smash unwary swimmers.

The Westin is a friendly place, (Their slogan is "You don't have to check-in to check us out!"), so before or after swimming, you can hire a carriage for a tour of the grounds or ride by gondola around the lagoon. Kids love it, and the cost is relatively inexpensive ($17 to hire the carriage and driver for 20 minutes or $2 for each person to ride in the gondola), and it gives you a reason to put your car in the hotel lot. Or, one of our favorite plans, enjoy the breakfast buffet at Prince Bill's and spend the rest of the morning on the beach!

Directions: Take Rice St through Lihue until you see the Harbor Village Shopping Center on your right. Park in the lot directly across the street, as close to the water as you can. Or, drive into the hotel, pass the main entrance, and take the second right. That road will take you to the beach access parking lot behind the newest of the hotel's three towers.

Hanama'ulu Beach

A perfect crescent of soft shining sand, the beach at Hanama'ulu Bay is perfect for building sandcastles and hunting sunrise shells. In summer, the waves are gentle enough for children to enjoy. Rolling to shore in long, even swells only about a foot or two high, they break into miniature crests which turn to layers of white foam flecked with sandy gold, like the lacy borders of a lovely shawl. Even the occasional "wipe-outs" were not serious because the sandy bottom slopes very gradually.

Children can chase lots of tiny sandcrabs, and there is plenty of shade for babies beneath the tall, graceful ironwood trees which fringe the sand. Behind the beach, the Hanama'ulu Stream forms shallow pools as it winds toward the bay, and the bottom is so firm that small children can wade, pulling toy trucks or cars behind them. Older ones can hunt for tiny crayfish and other river creatures to capture with nets. Local children like to scoot across the sandbar on handcrafted skim boards, disks of gaily colored, varnished plywood, or race their bikes along the bank and up improvised ramps in order to plunge them into the water where the stream is deeper. They also build enormous rafts of river plants and float with the current, which can begin to flow rapidly in a short time when the tide changes.

This spot behind the beach is quite beautiful. The deep gold of the river is shaded by trees so tall and dense you can hardly see the sky, and the dark green leaves trail into the water behind stalks of lavender water hyacinths, their petals streaked with the colors of peacock feathers. A picnic pavilion faces the river, and other tables look out over the beautiful curve of the bay. Everything is uncrowded, even the playground, as this beach is frequented by few tourists. Unfortunately, it is also in the path used by helicopters returning to the airport at the end of their scenic tours, and so you hear a lot of choppers. Try to ignore them, and also the semipermanent tents of campers. Plan your visit for the morning as the mosquitoes get hungry about 4 pm!

Directions: Turn off Rt 56 towards the sea at Hanama'ulu, just north of Lihue. Bear right at the fork and follow the road until it ends at the park.

Lydgate Beach Park

You can picnic, barbecue, or just come for the swimming at this wonderful family park just south of the Wailua River. It's a favorite spot for families on the island's eastern shore because it has something for everyone. A lava-rimmed pool provides safe swimming for babies and toddlers, even in winter months. Adjacent is an enormous lava-rimmed pool which breaks the surf into rolling swells excellent for swimming, rafting, and floats of all kinds. Here is one of the best snorkeling spots on the island, for many brightly colored fish feed along the rocky perimeter, and the rocky wall protects swimmers from dangerous currents. If you bring along some stale bread or crackers in a plastic bag, they will swim right up to you!

At Lydgate, you can also fly a kite, play frisbee on the wide, sandy beach, collect shells and driftwood, or just relax on the golden sand. There are showers for rinsing off sand and salt when you are ready to go home.

A nice walk northward takes you around the bay to the Wailua River which you can ford if the current is not too strong. Swimming in the brackish, calm water of the river is fun, although parents of young children should not let them stray from the edges because the water can become deep very quickly. Swimming where the river empties into the bay is not recommended because of dangerous, unpredictable currents and rip tides. If you walk in the opposite direction from the lava pools, the beach is almost deserted and you will have a spectacular view of the coastline, particularly when sunrise or sunset paints the sky with gold and orange, and deepens the blues of the ocean, bright with shining foam. The beach is perfect for walking, and the patterns of foam crossing the sand are the most lovely we have ever seen. You'll probably find only one or two people, probably fishermen checking their lines. Swim with caution, however, for the surf is rough and currents powerful; Lydgate's pools are much safer.

Directions: Take Leho Road off Rt 56 just north of the Wailua Golf Course. The turn to the park is clearly marked. Follow the road around to the left to get to the lava pools. If, however, you want to walk the long beach, take the first right turn instead. A long road runs along the beach, behind the Kaha Lani Condominiums and the golf course, and there are plenty of places to leave your car.

Kapa'a Beaches

The beaches at Kapa'a provide safe swimming for small children, except in times of heavy surf.Take Punihi Road opposite the Big Save on Rt 56, and drive towards the water. A small reef about 20 yards offshore makes a relatively safe swimming area almost the length of Kapa'a town, and it is usually full of small children splashing and babies playing in the shaded sand.

Kealia Beach

North of Kapa'a on Rt 56 and just past a scenic overlook turnout, you will see spectacular Ke'alia Beach, a long, wide curve of golden sand ending in a rocky point. When the surf is up, lots of surfers ride the long, even rollers. At low tide during summer months, the waves can be quite gentle, particularly at the far end of the beach where lava rocks extending into the sea create a cove where the water is quieter. Watch out, however, for the small, blue 'men 'o war' jellyfish which can be washed in by high surf. If you see them on the sand, they are probably also floating in the water! They pack a nasty sting, so go to another beach for the day! Firm, level sand makes this a perfect walking beach, and children will enjoy playing in the shallow pools behind the beach where a stream flows into the ocean. Plenty of parking is available off Rt 56.

Donkey Beach

Ringed by rolling pasture crisscrossed by wire fences, Donkey Beach takes it name from its gentle, four-footed neighbors. This is a lovely and peaceful spot, a long curve of sand which ends in piles of rock on both sides. The surf is strong, even in summer. The waves rise slowly; curl in long, even swells; crest with gleaming foam, and break straight down with thunderous explosions of spray. The rhythm is hypnotic—you could watch them form and crash for hours. We saw no one in the water, though—our first hint that Donkey Beach was for sun-worshipers rather than swimmers. We soon discovered that this beach is unique—the only one we've seen on Kauai where nudity is the rule. Those on the beach were not tourists, judging from their dark allover tans. Some were more covered up than others, so you won't feel out of place if you hang onto your suit. Otherwise bring along some sunblock for parts not normally exposed! Or you may regret your frolic in the altogether when you try to sit down later on!

Directions: You can no longer drive to Donkey Beach because the cane roads are gated and locked. However, about 3/4 mile north of the mile 11 marker on Rt 56, you will see cars parked on the shoulder, next to a well-worn path leading across the cane field to the beach. (The walk would take less than ten minutes). You can request a formal permit to cross private property to gain access to the beach (all beaches on Kauai are public) by stopping off during business hours at the Lihue Plantation office at 2970 Kele St in Lihue and filling out a short information form.

Anahola Bay

The beach at Anahola Bay is so long that to walk from one end to the other will take you almost an hour. The colors are magnificent, particularly as the sun is rising or in late afternoon as it moves to the west over the dark green mountains, deepening the blue of the water and the gold of the sand while brightening the tall white puff clouds until they seem to glow with light.

At the southern end of the bay, a state park provides barbecues, picnic tables, restrooms and showers, although over the last couple of years, campers have erected some rather permanent looking shelters which monopolize the shoreline. This end of the bay is sheltered by a rocky point, and the still, shallow water is often full of splashing toddlers and babies as well as older children learning to snorkel. Midway around the curve of the beach, the surf is strong and regular enough for riding, but the waves break with force and the currents are powerful most of the year. Further north, the waves are more gentle but the bottom becomes rocky. Local people like this spot for surf fishing, while their children play in the large shallow pools formed by the Anahola Stream as it winds toward the bay. The tadpoles, which our children had watched and hunted with such pleasure last summer, came early this year, and there were only a few stragglers left. The tiny river fish were harder to catch but fun in the trying, as were the small shrimp we discovered hiding by the grasses near the bank.

The children also enjoyed making voyages of discovery on their boogie boards where the stream was a bit deeper, and the boards came in handy one afternoon when, caught in a sudden passing rainshower, we used them to build a fort and pretended we were hiding out from monsters.

Anahola Bay is a favorite place for the whole family, and a good choice on weekends when other, more well known beaches become crowded. Watch out for the small, blue 'men o' war' jellyfish which are sometimes washed ashore after a storm. If you see them on the sand, go to another beach for the day, for the sting can be very painful.

A short drive (or long walk) north of the river will take you to a place where local people often snorkel and spear fish in about eight feet of water relatively protected from the surf by rock formations. Snorkeling is not advisable in high surf, particularly in winter months, because of strong, unpredictable currents.

For a picnic on the beach, stop at Duane's Ono Burger next to the Anahola Store just north of the turn off Rt 56 to the Beach Road. Though expensive, the burgers are imaginative creations, featuring various combinations of avocado, sprouts, vegetables, teriyaki, and various kinds of cheeses. But don't eat there; pack up and head for the beach! If possible, phone your order in ahead, for the staff can run low on manners during rush hour, and the waiting area can best be described as charmless.

Directions: To park at the spot were the waves are biggest, turn left off the Beach Road at the first right-of-way-to-beach sign. To park at the Anahola Stream, turn off Rt 56 at Aliomanu Road and follow it to the mouth of the stream.

North Shore
Beach Adventures

Moloa'a Bay

At the end of a well-graded, semi-paved road which winds for several miles through the lush green countryside, Moloa'a Bay's lovely curve of sandy beach is discovered by few tourists. As you follow the road through this quiet, rural landscape, you can hear wonderful sounds emerge from the stillness—the breeze rustling in the leaves, the chirping of insects, the snorting of horses grazing in tree-shaded meadows. At road's end, you will find a gate attached to an unfriendly looking barbed wire fence intended to discourage parking along the shoulder of the road. Walk through the gate and cross a winding, shallow stream, where our children discovered a thousand tadpoles apparently not informed that frog's eggs had hatched a month earlier everywhere else.

At this point the bay, hidden by the half dozen homes which ring the beach, suddenly comes into view—an almost dazzling half-moon of shining golden sand and turquoise water. The long, wide beach ends in grassy hills and piles of lava rocks on the left and a sheer cliff on the right. To the left, the rocks are fun to climb and search for shells and trapped fish, although this windward side of the bay is too rough for swimming and the bottom very rocky. To the right of the stream, the bay is more sheltered, with bright red and yellow catamarans pulled up on golden sand sprinkled with blue morning glories. Here the water is gentler and the bottom more sandy. In summer, swelling waves make excellent swimming for adults and children accompanied by adults. Snorkelers can swim out through the sandy corridor to the rockier part of the bay near the cliff, or float in the shallow water close to shore and dig in the sandy bottom for beautiful shells.

In times of heavy surf, however, this bay, like all windward beaches, can have dangerous currents and rip tides. Even during these times, though, Moloa'a Bay is a beautiful place for walking. The peaceful solitude is filled with the sound of waves. The crystal blue water, traced with the shadowy patterns of the rocks below, stretches out to the distant horizon where pale clouds fade into a limitless sky. At 5 pm you might see a dozen horses, wandering home after another difficult day of grazing, stop at the stream for a drink or a roll in the shallows—a spectacular sight with the setting sun glistening on the water and the horses darkening slowly to silhouettes.

Directions: Take Rt 56 to the Moloa'a Sunrise Fruit Stand just south of Kilauea. Turn right on Kuamo'o Road, then right again at Moloa'a Road and follow it to the end.

Larsen's Beach

Getting to Larsen's Beach is half the fun. A right-of-way-to-beach road wanders through pastureland, where horses grazing peacefully seem sketched into a landscape portrait of meadows silvery green with waving grasses, trees and mountains in richer, darker shades, and the sky light blue with masses of white, shining clouds. At the end of the well-graded, sandy road is a small parking area and a gate leading to the top of the cliff, where the beach below seems a slender ribbon of white against the dark blue water. Although a second, smaller gate seems to direct you to the right, walking through it takes you to a steep path ending in rocks. Instead, walk down the hillside to the left on a well worn path with a gentle slope. Even our six-year-old had little difficulty managing the descent or the climb back up. In fact, he accepted the job of trailblazer and earned a "pathfinder" badge for leading us back up the the car again! A five-minute walk down the slope brings you to a long, lovely beach curving along the coastline and disappearing around a distant bend—perfect for lazy afternoons of beachcombing and exploring.

Although a rocky reef extending about 70 yards offshore seems to invite swimming and snorkeling, Larsen's Beach is one of the most dangerous on the island. Before you begin the hike down, observe the ocean carefully and locate the channel through the reef, just to the left of the rocky point where you are standing. The churning water caused by the swift current makes the channel easiest to see from this height, and once noted, it can be recognized at sea level. Once you see this channel, you can also pick out the smaller channels which cut through the reef at several other points. Swimmers and snorkelers should avoid going near any of these channels, particularly the large one, because currents can be dangerously strong and even turn into a whirlpool when the tide is going out. Remember, Larsen's Beach has no lifeguard, and help is not close by. Currents can be exceptionally treacherous at any time, but particularly in winter months, and swimmers drown here almost every year. The watchword is caution: swim in pairs, never go out beyond the reef, try to stay within 15 yards of the shore, and examine the surface of the water carefully to avoid swimming near a channel. If you snorkel, stay where you can stand up at will, and don't get so absorbed in looking at the fish that you lose track of where you are. Have the judgment not to go out at all if surf conditions don't seem right to you.

A trip to Larsen's Beach does not require swimming or snorkeling. If you bring reef-walking sneakers to protect your feet, you can walk around in the shallow water and watch colorful fish who don't seem afraid of people. Or walk for miles along the magnificent coastline of this picture-perfect beach. Hunt for shells, or simply lose yourself in the spectacle of nature's beauty. You will probably encounter only another person or two. The drive back is wonderful, with spectacular views of the rolling hills, lined by fences and stands of trees, and beyond them the dark and majestic mountains reaching to touch the clouds.

Directions: Take Rt 56 to the Moloa'a Sunrise Fruit Stand just south of Kilauea, and turn right onto Kuamo'o Road. Go past the Moloa'a Road turnoff for about 1.1 miles and look for a dirt road on the right. The right turn will be very sharp, and then almost immediately another beach access sign will mark the left turn onto the long, straight road to the beach. Follow to the end, and walk downhill to the left.

Kilauea Bay

If you've ever had the fantasy of searching through the jungle to find a remote and hidden paradise, Kilauea Bay should be your destination. The road to this unspoiled beach tests the mettle of both car and driver with new challenges at practically every turn. Deeply rutted, even gouged in places by ditches and holes, it can turn into a quagmire in rain, but in dry weather, it can be navigated without too much difficulty by a careful driver even in a rented subcompact. Pick a dry day, and the road will add the zest of adventure and heighten the excitement of discovering, just beyond the last ditch and bunches of trailing vegetation, a bay shaped like a perfect half-moon, the deep blue water sparkling with light and the golden sand outstretched between two rocky bluffs like a tawny cat sleeping in the sun.

To get to the beach, you must wade across the Kilauea Stream which winds into the bay through dunes built up by the changing tides. The mouth of the stream changes shape each year. One year it may be shallow enough for small children to manage at low tide, but at other times you'll have to carry your youngsters on your shoulders. The width can vary from a few yards to a hundred, and during stormy times when the stream floods, crossing may be difficult, even impossible. To the left of the stream, the beach ends abruptly in an old rock quarry, the original purpose for the road and now a great spot for pole fishing. To the right of the stream, the sandy beach extends a long way before ending in piles of lava rocks which children will enjoy climbing and exploring for tidal pools. Chances are you'll encounter only another person or two and can watch in solitude as the waves roll towards the beach in long, even swells, break into dazzling white crests, and rush towards shore in layers of gold and white foam.

Although the surf can be dangerously strong and the currents treacherous at certain times, particularly in winter when the beach may almost disappear beneath the crashing waves, we found the swimming safe enough in summer for our nine and eleven-year-olds to surf on their boogie boards in the shallow water, although even close to shore the pull of the undertow made us watch them closely. The tiny blue Portuguese 'men o' war' are sometimes washed ashore here after a storm, so if you see any on the sand, go to another beach, for these small jellyfish pack a giant sting!

Behind the beach, the stream forms brackish pools where children can swim safely, except near the stream's entrance into the bay where the current can be swift, particularly at high tide. Last August, the pools were wider than we had ever seen, like a shallow lagoon, and our family had a great time netting hundred of tadpoles. Our children preferred this beach to almost any other because of the variety of things they could do and the challenge of ripping the leaves off the branches that scraped the sides of the car as we maneuvered around the gullies on the way down and back. We loved the beach because we had it all to ourselves.

Directions: At Kilauea, turn off Rt 56 onto Kolo Road, then turn left onto Kilauea Road, and drive through the town. After you pass the Kong Lung store, take the second dirt road on the right. Follow it about a mile to the end. On the way back, stop in at Jacques's Bakery on Oka Street for some fresh wheat and molasses bread and coconut danish pastries.

Secret Beach

Secret Beach is one of those rare and special places where the world can be forgotten, where you can feel, for a few hours, as if you were alone at the beginning of time. The colors are brilliant, and the breeze is fresh and tangy with salt. The ocean reaches out to touch the sky at an endless horizon, and the crashing of waves is all you can hear. As you walk, you will leave the only footprints on warm, golden sand shining brilliantly in the sun.

Nestled at the base of a sheer cliff just north of Kilauea, Secret Beach is well off the beaten track for good reason. You must hike down (and back up!) a rocky trail which zigzags through trees, gullies, and brush. You can drive only to the trail's beginning, after taking a dirt road which seems to end at the gate of a farm, then veers sharply to the right along a goat pasture, before stopping abruptly, apparently in nowhere. A small, weathered sign announces the beginning of the 'Beach Trail,' which warns of the condition of the path down and at the same time reassures you that others have made the trip before! The narrow path runs quite close to a barbed wire fence, but a short uphill walk will bring you to the top of the trail down. From here, you can hear the waves crashing below—apparently not very far away—which is reassuring as you look down on a trail which seems to disappear into a tangle of jungle. The path is steep in places—sneakers are a good idea—but branches, roots, and vines offer plenty of handholds, and if you're out of shape, you can always resort to the seat of your pants!

The walk down will take about seven minutes, just long enough to whet your appetite for a glimpse of that surf you can only hear. You'll even feel rather daring as the path makes the last sharp plunge before leveling off to the sand, and you can see, at last, through a screen of palm trees and hanging vines, a magnificent stretch of golden sand and a shining turquoise sea. In rainy times, this enormous triangle of sand may be partly covered by a lagoon fed by a stream winding down behind the beach. You can walk in either direction. To the left, you can climb a rocky outcropping and find a small beach ending in a steep cliff. A house or two perched atop the cliff will startle you, although the cliff is too sheer for any trail down. To the right of the beach trail, you can walk a long way across the sand and perhaps explore some small caves etched by the waves into the base of the cliff.

Secret Beach is not a place to come alone, for the obvious reason of its isolation. And swimming is not a good idea. The surf is rough, and the current strong and unpredictable,and you'd never find a lifeguard if you were caught in an undertow. In fact, during the winter, this beach, enormous as it is, can disappear almost entirely under huge, crashing waves. Instead of swimming, you can walk along the water's edge, hunt for shells, and forget everything but the feel of wet sand between your toes.

The walk back up the cliff will give you time to adjust to the world you left behind—just about 10 minutes of mild exertion, with the air cool under the trees and the leaves speckled with sunlight. This would not be a pleasant hike in the mud, though, so plan your adventure with an eye to the weather and don't go after a soaking rain. By the time you reach your car and remember that you have to stop at the store for chocolate milk, the peaceful solitude you left behind will be as hard to recapture as a wave rippling on the sand.

But for a few moments, you were lost forever to your working-day world. This may be the secret of Secret Beach, and it is a secret worth keeping.

Directions: Drive north of Kilauea on Rt 56. Turn right onto a dirt road .3 mile north of Kolo Road, just a few feet beyond a highway sign indicating a right turnoff Rt 56. Follow the road until it ends at the sign "Beach Trail." The rest is up to you! Note: One reader discovered another secret about this beach, when she and her family reached the bottom of the trail and ran into "a long-haired young man wearing nothing but a guitar!" So be prepared for strange music!

Kalihiwai Bay

You'll catch your first glimpse of Kalihiwai Bay as you drive down the narrow road carved into the side of the sheer cliff which encloses it on one side. From the side, the bay is a perfect semi-circle of blue, rimmed with shining white sand and nestled between two lava cliffs. Ironwood trees ring the beach and behind them, across the sandy road, several homes peek out at the sea. A clear, freshwater stream flows into the bay near the far end, so shallow and gentle at low tide that small children can splash around safely. It becomes deep enough behind the beach to be the departure point for royak excursions, although swimming is not recommended in the river itself.

One of our favorite family beaches, Kalihiwai Bay offers wonderful summertime fun for people of all ages. Little ones will love the shallow pools behind the beach where they can fish or float on rafts. Ocean swimming is terrific too! The waves rise very slowly and break in long, even crests over a sloping sandy bottom, perfect for wave jumping and boogie boarding. One day we watched a dozen children celebrate a birthday with a surfing party. In winter, when the surf is up, it's a favorite spot for local surfers. However, particularly during stormy weather, the surf and currents in the bay become formidable. At those times, it's a lovely beach for walking, with firm sand and magnificent views of the cliffs.

Directions: A yellow siren atop a pole just south of the beach is a reminder of the *tsunami* or tidal wave of 1946 which washed away the bridge originally linking the two roads to the bay. Both are still marked Kalihiwai Road at their separate intersections with Rt 56. Either one will take you to the bay, although if you choose the Kalihiwai Road just north of the long bridge on Rt 56, you'll have to wade across the stream's mouth in order to reach the beach. The Kalihiwai Road south of the bridge and just north of Kilauea winds through the countryside before curving down the steep cliff on the southern edge of the bay.

Sunset Beach

Just north of Kalihiwai, on the other side of a rocky cliff, is a small secluded beach perfect for hunting shells. The reason is the reef which makes the bottom too rocky for good swimming. But the walking is wonderful, and the pieces of coral and bits of shells will delight the eye and fill the pockets. It's also a quiet place for reflecting and daydreaming.

Directions: Turn off Rt 56 at the northernmost Kalihiwai Road, turn left onto Anini Road and then take the first right turn, just before the road curves to the left. Follow the curving sandy lane through the grapetrees until you see the beach.

Anini Beach

At the edge of Anini Road, you will find miles of white sandy beach protected by a reef. At some places the beach road is so close to the water that you could almost jump in, and it is a beautiful drive. A beach park offers restrooms and picnic facilities, although you can turn off the road at almost any spot, park between the stately ironwoods, and find your private paradise. Snorkeling can be good, although the water is very shallow. Across the road, the Kauai Polo Club hosts polo matches on summer Sunday afternoons at 2 pm.

The road then passes through a quiet residential area, and, near the end, a stream flows into the sea. A sandbar extending quite far out invites wading and fishing. Children love the quiet water and the tiny beautiful shells which are plentiful along the waterline. The scene is so peaceful that you can hear amazing sounds: the roar of the surf as it breaks on the reef far offshore, and near your feet, the gentle rippling of the sea upon the sand.

If you begin your sunset drive to Hanalei too late to reach there before dark, you can watch the sun set into the ocean at Anini Beach, a glorious sight which can be yours in perfect solitude. The tall ironwood trees darken to feathery silhouettes against a pale gray and orange sky, filled with lines of puff clouds. The water shimmers gold as the sun's dying fire fades slowly to a pearl and smoky gray, to the songs of crickets and the lapping of gentle waves.

Hanalei Bay

Famous for its spectacular beauty, Hanalei Bay is a long half-moon of sandy beach carved into the base of a sheer cliff on one side and narrowing into a rocky point on the other. Several Trans-Pacific Cup Races from California to Hawaii end in this natural harbor, and during summer months, gaily colored boats rock gently at anchor on the leeward, eastern side where the Hanalei stream flows into the bay. Near the marina, a small park provides picnic facilities and restrooms. Turn right off Rt 560 onto Weke Road, then right onto Aku Road. The park pavilion will be on your left. You don't really need the park, however, as you can park near the beach by following almost any road off Rt 560 towards the water. The biggest breakers crest near the center of the curving coastline, where you will most likely see surfers hunting the perfect ride, although during winter months the surf can become too dangerous. In fact, boats are moved out of the bay by mid-October, and by winter, twenty-foot waves are not uncom-mon. Keep that in mind as you consider a zodiac adventure!

At any time of year, Hanalei Bay is fantastic for frisbee, the wide sandy beach firm and level for hard running. If you get hungry from all this exercise, look for the green Tropical Taco truck usually parked near the Hanalei Dolphin Restaurant, just north of the bridge over the Hanalei River. West of the little town of Hanalei, still a cluster of weatherbeaten buildings and quaint churches, are several beautiful places, and you can explore almost any road turning off towards the water and discover a lovely spot. At the westernmost curve of the bay, you'll find a calm, protected beach where the water is relatively quiet even when most of the north shore is too rough for safe swimming. At these times, the number of cars alongside the road will show you where to park!

Lumahai Beach

The setting for the Bali Hai scenes in the movie South Pacific, Lumahai Beach is stunningly beautiful, a curve of white sand nestled at the base of a dark lava cliff, with a giant lava rock jutting out of the turquoise sea just offshore. Getting there requires a trek down from the roadside through slippery mud (showers are frequent on the Hanalei side of the island), and the trip back up is even worse, especially if you have to carry a tired child. If there are toddlers in your family, you might consider hiring a babysitter or buying a postcard! Swimming at Lumahai Beach is dangerous, particularly during winter when surf is rough and powerful. There is no reef to offer protection from the unpredictable currents and rip tides which make Lumahai Beach notorious as one of the most treacherous on the island. Beware also climbing that spectacular offshore rock for a photograph, as a sudden powerful wave can easily knock you off!

At the other end of Lumahai, about a mile further west, is a beach with some of the biggest breakers we found, and a sign warns against swimming in winter because of high surf and strong currents. The stream which flows into the sea here is ice cold from mountain rainwater, a refreshing way to rinse off sand and salt. After the waves break and the foam washes over the sandy spit at the stream's mouth, miniature waves form and roll across the shallows for children to enjoy in summer months. There is no shade for babies near the water, however.

The stream meets the ocean at a huge rocky bluff, a spectacular place to sit quietly and watch the waves crash against the rocks, sending dazzling spray into the air. It is also a beautiful beach for walking, although the coarse sand is hard going except near the waterline, and you must cross a vast expanse of hot sand to get from the parking area to the sea. Bring sandals! You can hunt for striped scallop shells shining in the sun, or wander all the way to the rocky bluff that separates this part of Lumahai Beach from the part pictured in all the postcards. Trying to cross the rocks would

be hazardous, however, even at low tide, due to the occasional "killer wave" which can come up suddenly out of nowhere and smash you into the rocks. A small cave etched into the base of the cliff with a floor of powder soft, cool sand is a perfect spot for daydreaming and wave-watching, preferably with someone special.

Directions: Drive north of Hanalei on Rt 560 and look for the mile 4 marker. You'll see a lot of cars parked on a shoulder just past a 25 mph speed zone sign. Park on the right, opposite a No Passing Zone sign, lock up, and begin the hike down. To get to the western end of Lumahai, drive to the mile 5 marker, look for an emergency telephone by the road, and turn into a sandy parking area under the trees and beside the stream.

Ha'ena Beach Park

An icy stream winds across this lovely golden sand beach curving along the coastline. The water is a dazzling blue. An offshore reef provides summertime snorkeling and makes the waves gentle for swimming and rafting. Restrooms, showers, picnic and barbecue facilities are available, and camping is permitted. You might even find a sandwich truck if you forget to bring lunch! You can walk a long way in both directions, with spectacular views of the towering cliffs and shimmering sea.

Tunnels Beach

You'll see lessons in snorkeling and scuba diving at Tunnels Beach because the water is usually so calm. Tunnels is protected by two reefs, the outer reef favored by surfers for the perfect arcs that give this beach its name, and the inner reef a wonderful place to explore for fish and sea life. Tunnels is about the only beach on the north shore that is usually calm enough for beginners, although even here you may find rough surf and treacherous currents during winter months. Listen to the surf reports and plan any winter visits for low tide!

In summertime, you can bring the kids and let them paddle about on boogie boards while the older ones try their luck with mask and snorkel. Bring a plastic baggie of frozen peas, release them one at a time and you'll be surrounded by fish who think the peas are an exotic yuppie seaweed! Swimming through the coral formations of the reef, which is almost like a maze of tunnels, can be great fun when the water is quiet. Enter the reef through the sandy channel on the right, and hundreds of fish in rainbow colors will swim right up to your mask. If the showers which frequent the north shore rain on your parade, you can take shelter under the ironwood trees—or under your boogie board!

Tunnels can get crowded, particularly in summer. The beach is the departure point for Captain Zodiac boat tours, and both swimmers and the boats have to share the only sandy channel out to the reef. Though the zodiac staff may try to motion you out of the channel to make way for the boats, don't be intimidated! People—not boats—have the right of way.

Between May and August, the area between the two reefs may look calm enough for safe swimming. Watch out, however, for either of these danger signs: high surf on the outer reef or fast moving ripples in the channel between the reefs—indications of powerful, swift currents that could sweep you out into open ocean. At those times, hunt for shells on the beach instead of swimming, or walk around the rocks to the east, where you may find some sunbathers with very dark tans in all the best places!

Directions: On Rt 560, drive 1.1 miles west of the entrance to Charo's at the Hanalei Colony Resort. You will pass the mile 8 marker and the turnoff to the YMCA camp. At one time, you could park close to the beach, but now the landowner has fenced the area off. Just look for all the cars on the shoulder, get as close as you can, and walk in. No public facilities.

Ke'e Beach

When you can drive no further on Rt 560 on Kauai's north shore, you will discover a beach so beautiful you won't quite believe it to be real. The Na Pali cliffs rise like dark green towers behind the golden sand, and a reef extending out from shore creates a peaceful lagoon ideal for summertime swimming. As you walk along the shining sand, new cliffs come into view until the horizon is filled with their astonishing shapes and you begin to imagine princesses held captive in enchanted castles.

Like all windward beaches on the north shore, the surf at Ke'e Beach varies with the seasons. Winter surf can reach 20 feet, and then the ocean roars with crashing waves and churning foam with undercurrents far too strong for safe swimming. In summer, however, the turquoise water can be perfectly still and so clear that bubbles on the surface cast shadows on the sandy bottom.

Snorkeling can be spectacular close to the reef, even in the shallow water where you can stand up at will, and the water, warmed by the sun, will feel ice cold along the surface from rainwater. The coral reef is shallow enough to walk on, but you'll need sneakers to protect your feet from coral cuts. Be careful too of unpredictable currents in the channel to the left of the reef, as they can be strong enough to pull a swimmer out of this sheltered area into the open sea.

Large trees at the beach provide shade for babies and protection from the occasional rainshowers which cool the air and make the coastline sparkle. Small children can play and swim safely in the shallow water or climb over the rocks at low tide. Bring nets and pails for small fishermen! They will also love collecting limpet shells or the tops of spiral shells. Because of an unusual combination of low tide and calm summer sea, we were able to walk west across the rocks and around the point for the first time in more than six years. From this vantage point, the Na Pali cliffs are truly magnificent—jutting into the cobalt blue ocean in vivid green ridges, the surf crashing in thundering sprays of foam. This walk is too dangerous to attempt in any but the calmest sea, and you must watch the direction of the tide carefully so that your return trip does not involve crossing slippery rocks through crashing waves. Ke'e Beach, lovely as it looks, can have treacherous currents and unpredictable surf, and so extra caution is a must. Showers and restrooms are available. If possible come early and come midweek, for parking at this lovely and popular spot is hard to come by, especially in summer.

Beach Safety

We describe the beaches in their summer mood, when the surf and currents can be at their most gentle. From mid-October to mid-April, however, swimmers must be particularly cautious on the windward beaches to the north and northeast where the surf and currents are more unpredictable and dangerous. Plan your beach adventures according to surf conditions (Call 245-6001 for a report on the size of the swell and the times of high and low tides).

A few simple suggestions: Don't swim alone or too far out at a beach where the currents and tides are unfamiliar, and avoid swimming where a river flows into the sea. Should you ever find yourself caught in a strong undertow or rip tide, and if your efforts to free yourself are not successful, remember this: don't panic, conserve your energy and drift with the current until it weakens. These currents usually weaken beyond the point where the waves break, and many are shaped like horseshoes, so that at some point you will probably be able to swim back in. You'll find the safest snorkeling in the rock enclosed pool at Lydgate Park on the eastern shore, or at sheltered Poipu Beach to the south. If you want to surf, watch where the local surfers ride the waves. They know where the currents should be avoided.

Beware of walking or even standing close to the edge of cliffs or rocks to photograph the pounding surf, as waves vary in size and strength and a huge one may come up suddenly and wash your camera away—perhaps you along with it! These sudden large waves can be treacherous because they are unexpected as well as powerful, particularly on northern and western beaches where there are no reefs to protect against strong ocean currents.

The Portuguese 'man o' war', a tiny blue jellyfish, packs a huge walloping sting in its long, trailing tentacle. These creatures sometimes dot the waterline after they have been washed ashore by heavy surf. Don't step on them or pick them up. If you are stung while swimming, pull the jellyfish off carefully, trying not to touch the stinger any more than you have to, or use some sand to scrape the stinger off. Meat tenderizer is sometimes used as a poultice to help break down the poison. The best medicine, however, is prevention. If you see them on the sand, pack up and head out for another beach! An even smaller critter, the bacterium leptospirosis, has been found in Kauai's rivers and streams, so avoid fresh-water swimming if you have open cuts or sores.

Instead, swim in the ocean or the brackish water near where a stream flows into the sea.

On Kauai, as anywhere, follow normal rules of self-protection: Lock your car against theft as you would at home, and avoid walking alone at night in unlit, deserted areas—including those romantic beaches.

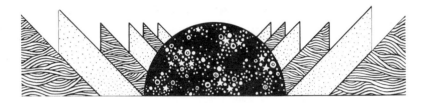

Beware the Hawaiian Sun

If you lie out in the sun between 11:30 am and 2:30 pm, you will fry like a pancake, even in a half hour, because Hawaii lies close to the equator and the sun is exceedingly strong. Even on cloudy days, ultraviolet rays can cause a burn. The best sunscreens contain PABA, although this ingredient can give some people a rash. Some of the new 'paba-free' sunscreens are also highly effective. Choose 'waterproof' rather than 'water-resistant' lotions, though don't put too much faith in the manufacturers' claims! Even waterproof sunscreens wash off in salt water and should be re-applied after an hour—or two hours at the most. Keep an eye on your child's skin, and bring a t-shirt (the most reliable sun-protection!), especially for after-swimming sandcastle projects! Dermatologists we have consulted find little improvement in protection between a lotion rated SPF 15 and one rated SPF 35 , and some would recommend the #15 because it has a lower concentration of chemicals.

We've had good results with Johnson and Johnson's Sundown, which forms a skin-like coating that seems good for about two hours. A paba-free sunblock gel with the strange name "Bullfrog" (available in island pharmacies and sports stores) is effective for lips, noses, and cheeks. Since children are so easily sunburned, you might schedule family beach visits for the early morning or late afternoon, and plan meals, naps, or drives for the noonday hours. Sunburns are not often fully visible until it is too late, but you can check your child's skin by pressing it with your finger. If it blanches dramatically, get the child a shirt or consider calling it a day. Keep an extra lotion in the car, for without lotion, it's not worth going to the beach!

For babies, a complete sunblock like Coppertone Supershade #15 is essential since their skin lacks the melanin, which produces tanning, until they are about 9 months old. A hat will protect the scalp; use lotion everywhere else, even on feet! Babies should stay out of the noonday sun and in the shade as much as possible at other times (take an umbrella to the beach). Many dermatologists currently recommend that children use SPF 15, or at least not less than SPF 8. For spots which kids rub often, like right under the eyes, you can use Bullfrog or Chapstick #15. It's a good idea to make a firm rule that kids get "greased up" before leaving for the beach as they hate to stand still once the sand is in sight!

Restaurants

Notes

Westside Restaurants

The Green Garden

There has been a Green Garden Restaurant for about as long as Kauai has been called the Garden Island. A local legend, it has been owned and operated by the same family since 1948, and it still bases its reputation on generous portions and inexpensive prices. The menu features American, Japanese, and Chinese dinners, many priced below $5. Even at lunch the meals include several courses as well as a beverage. Service is fast and very friendly at the long, ranch style tables, and although the dining room may look and sound more like a high school cafeteria than a garden, you certainly get full value for your money. Where else could you find a hamburger platter with fries, a salad, dessert, and iced tea for under $4? At $5.50, the fresh ulua tempura or shrimp tempura are also bargains. For children, club sandwiches are about $4, and grilled cheese only $1.95—remember: this price includes salads plain enough for picky eaters, lots of fries and a drink!

The pies, though, would stand out at any price, and we recommend them all—the chocolate cream pie is a child's favorite treat, and the coconut cream pie has a light flaky crust filled with marvelously light egg custard topped with toasted coconut. The macadamia nut cream pie is equally delicious. The lilikoi chiffon pie, for which the Green Garden is justifiably famous, has the lightest texture imaginable and a taste of passion fruit that will arouse your taste buds.

Try to avoid arriving for lunch at noon, when tour buses frequently pull into the lot. But even if you're caught in the crush, your service will not suffer because this staff has group service down to a science. Granted that food quality is affected by the high volume, and that the pace is a bit hectic, the Green Garden is terrific for large families on small budgets. Children are treated with tolerance, and when parents give up efforts to make them sit still at the table, youngsters can play with the video games on the enclosed porch. The Green Garden also serves dinner, with almost the same entrees priced about $1 higher than lunch.

On Rt 50 in Hanapepe. Reservations suggested for dinner. 335-5422. Breakfast 7 am-11 am. Lunch 11 am-2 pm. Dinner 5 pm-8:30 pm. Closed Tuesday nights. Credit cards.

Wrangler's Restaurant

From the time you step across the wood plank floor into what looks like the set for that unfilmed Gunsmoke episode where Matt Dillon finally proposes to Kitty over a thick, juicy steak, you know that at Wrangler's, size is important. Everything is large. French fries come heaping on the plate. Seafood salad is a huge mound of crab, shrimp, scallops, olives and tomatoes. The "Wrangler Burger" fills the plate, and like the six other types of half-pound hamburgers ($2.75 to $4.75) includes soup or salad, as well as chips and salsa or french fries. The menu itself is enormous. You'll find Mexican dishes, plate lunches, sandwiches, and steaks, as well as Korean ribs and teriyaki. At dinner, you can choose from 9 steaks, including a 20 ounce sirloin or t-bone for $15.50, 12 seafood and 7 Mexican dinners. And for all this size, prices are reasonable, starting at $5.95 for a hamburger steak dinner.

This menu fits the theme of big steers and hearty appetites. The dining room has a deliberately straightforward look, with old tools and saddles hung on the white-washed wood walls, as if to foster your belief that only the guys in the white hats eat here. Blue vinyl tablecloths and gingham curtains fit right in with the theme of square meals and honest deals. Juke boxes with titles from thirty years ago sit silent, waiting, perhaps, for a 1950's quarter to make them come to life.

Quantity is clearly more important than quality. The Mexican food is tasty, but the meat could be better trimmed. Soup is served in a big bowl, but the seasoning is hasty and overly salty. Ribs with kim chee could have been less fatty. Chicken was crispy and moist, but the overly salty teriyaki sauce should be left on the side, if not in the kitchen! The generous ono filet ($8.50 lunch platter) tasted bitter from the grill, and the brown mushroom sauce which fortunately was confined in a small bowl, helped the otherwise tasteless white rice much more the fish! The best bet is the hamburgers, perfectly cooked, and served with lettuce and tomato on a soft kaiser roll.

The restaurant is perched on the main street of sleepy Waimea in the historic AKO Building. You'll see police officers and lots of other local people in the roomy booths along the walls. If you are exploring the island's westside, where you have few choices for provisions, Wrangler's is a good place to stop; but driving to Wrangler's for almost an hour from the east or south shores might make sense only if you were a paniolo herding cows—and if you like Marlboros too, for we found no non-smoking area!

Rt 50 in Waimea. Credit cards. Open Mon-Thurs 10:30 am to 9 pm; on Fri and Sat until 10 pm. 338-1218. Milk or coffee $.75.

Aloha Frappe

Blend 1/2 papaya, 1 banana, 1/2 cup fresh pineapple chunks or pineapple juice, guava nectar to keep the blender running smoothly (you can add rum or vodka to make a terrific cocktail)!

Midori Sunset

Pour 2 oz Midori Melon Liqueur and 1 oz vodka over ice. Fill glass with orange juice and stir, or if you prefer, mix in a blender. The honeydew flavor of the liqueur is also terrific with pineapple and coconut juice.

Fresh Fish With Rice

Place a steak, about 1" thick, in a casserole with butter. Add 1/2 cup mayonnaise and 1/4 cup soy sauce. Cover and bake 20-30 minutes at 350 degrees.

South Shore Restaurants

The Beach House Restaurant

A longtime favorite of both residents and visitors, the Beach House once perched on a sea wall only inches from the waves, a great spot to watch the sun set into the ocean and enjoy perfectly cooked seafood in a relaxed and casual setting. In fact, the tables were so close to the waves, that when Hurricane I'wa struck Kauai in 1982, the entire restaurant was swept out to sea — leaving only the concrete slab to mark the spot where so many evenings had passed so pleasantly.

One of the original owners has rebuilt the restaurant on the old site, at a more respectful distance from the waves. Sliding glass doors open to the evening air and to spectacular views of surfers catching the waves as the sun sets into the shimmering sea. As you stroll along the walkway next to the ocean, you will find it hard to believe that tables were once as close to the rocks as your feet!

Although the new building preserves the original restaurant's casual ambiance (waitpersons wear shorts), the dining room is far more elegant. White lattice and leafy plants give the impression of a gazebo by the sea. Pink tables with green cloths and comfortable upholstered chairs are arranged in a tiered L-shaped room, where fly fans hum pleasantly to encourage evening breezes.

The menu features steak and seafood dinners, which include salad and potato or rice. Prices have gone up, with steaks now among the least expensive entrees at $16.50, and the most expensive, lobster tail, a whopping $27.50. A unique feature, you can combine almost any two entrees into a dinner portion. Most wines cost $20 or more, with a Sterling Sauvignon Blanc fairly priced at $24. Since our bottle arrived barely cool, consider ordering when you sit down and start the bottle chilling in an ice bucket!

When the new Beach House first opened, we were disappointed in the combination dinners, where the small portions of steak and fish are more difficult to cook. Since then, we have tried full-size entrees and were much more pleased. The fresh ono ($18.50), was moist and flaky. If you ask to have the fish sauteed in plain butter, with the rather strongly flavored sauce and capers left on the side (or even better, in the kitchen!), you'll be able to enjoy its delicate flavor. A new entree, rack of lamb ($22.50), served in six separately grilled chops, was tender and juicy, though disappointingly bitter from the grill.

Dinners include a green salad, topped with a layer of grated romana cheese and a rather vinegary house dressing, and some overly sweet apple spice muffins. A strange combination of tastes, and we still wonder why the tables are not set with bread plates. Entrees are served with steamed rice, rice pilaf, french fries or baked potato, and a serving of vegetables.

Children will like the Beach House. They get crayons and paper for doodling while waiting for their steak, fish, or chicken ($6.50). After dinner, they can run around on the lawn outside or toss stones into the water while their parents linger over coffee.

When you make your reservation, be sure to ask for a window table and insist on it when you arrive. The Beach House has one of the most beautiful settings you can imagine, one of the few spots that is lovely even in the dark. Dinner can be truly special when you can sit by the window and enjoy the evening breezes as the last light of sunset fades and the waves begin to glisten with moonlight.

On Spouting Horn Road in Poipu. Reservations recommended. Request a window table, but be prepared to wait for it. 742-7575. Credit cards. Cocktails from 4 pm. Dinner 5:30-10:30 pm. House wine: William Wycliff $5.75/$10.25. Coffee/brewed decaf $1.

Brennecke's Beach Broiler

Brennecke's serves the best reasonably-priced fresh seafood on the island, and there are usually four varieties to choose from. It's worth calling ahead to find out what's going to be on the menu and reserving a portion of ulu'a or onaga if available so that you won't be disappointed to find it sold out when you arrive.

In this second story restaurant across the street from Poipu Beach Park, you'll find prices modest and the atmosphere decidedly informal, so you'll feel comfortable no matter what you're wearing. But the informal ambiance is the result of the meticulous attention to detail which enhances every aspect of the dining experience. The decor, for example, looks very plain—a porch in soft grey and white tones—but everything is spanking clean, the paint still shiny and fresh looking, the chairs and grey formica tables immaculate, the flowers in the window boxes bright and cheerful. It's the kind of porch where your child could retrieve a piece of pasta from the floor and put it in his mouth and you wouldn't have to look the other way. The food receives equal attention to detail. The clam chowder ($2.50) is creamy rather than thick, generous with clams, and delicately seasoned. Teriyaki steak stix ($5.95) is another delicious appetizer—medium rare, tasty, and sizzling hot. For entrees, the menu offers beef, pasta, and poultry, but the fresh seafood is the reason to come to Brennecke's. Your fish will be perfectly cooked, crisp on the outside, meltingly moist and delicious inside. The secret to Brennecke's flawless broiling is the grill, designed by owner Bob French and fueled by charcoal made from kiawe wood from Ni'ihau. It burns extremely hot and clean, quickly sealing in juices and leaving no aftertaste.

During our visits to Brennecke's over the years, we have sampled almost every fresh fish and have always been delighted. Even the old standbys, ahi and ono ($17.75), are so perfectly cooked that they seem extraordinary. Most recently, we tried opakapaka , a superb filet which could not have been juicier or tastier. Grouper, or white sea bass, with a texture somewhat like lobster, was also sensational, flaking easily and gently seasoned. If you are lucky, you will be able to sample the fresh mahi mahi, flaky   and soft, unforgettably sweet and garnished with homemade tartar sauce. Sixteen entrees include steak, chicken, and ribs, as well as combinations. Your dinner will arrive with delicious pasta and sauteed fresh vegetables, still crisp and vivid in color.

The wine list is limited, with almost all selections both inexpensive and ordinary, including a Brennecke's label Chardonnay (by Belvedere) for $10.95 which you will find sitting on your table when you arrive. You might try Brennecke's famous Mai Tai instead. Children can choose from 6 dinners ($4.95-$7.95) and even have chocolate milk ($1.25) or a grown-up looking fruit punch ($1.50). Kid's burgers, chicken, and fish are very successful, judging from the enthusiasm of 6 youngsters seated next to our table. If you're not hungry enough for a full dinner, Brennecke's is a great place to come for pu pus. No fewer than 14 varieties of munchies are available ($3-$7), including several sandwich baskets, nachos and burgers around $6. Ligea's BBQ beef ribs ($11.25/entree) can be ordered in an appetizer-sized portion of two ribs, each meaty and meltingly tasty.

Or you can bring the family for lunch after a hard morning of boogie boarding. Brennecke's "beach burgers" ($5.95) are delicious. Don't pass up the kiawe-broiled fresh fish sandwich ($7.50) which is wonderfully juicy and tasty. As you eat, you can watch the waves rolling to the sand across the street at Poipu Beach Park.

For the best in fresh fish, beautifully broiled and attractively served, you won't find a better spot than Brennecke's. The staff is friendly and professional, the dining comfortably open to evening breezes. Prices are reasonable, and best of all, you can be assured that your money will buy top quality.

Ho'one Rd. Poipu. For the daily fish report, or for reservations (necessary) 742-7588. Credit cards. House wine: Robert Mondavi red $4.25/$7.95 or William Wycliffe chablis $3.75/$7. A sign of the times: nine non-alcoholic "mocktails." Coffee or brewed decaf $1. Lunch 11:30 am-3 pm. Dinner 5-10:30 pm daily. Happy hour 2 pm-4 pm daily.

Brick Oven Pizza

We had heard about Brick Oven Pizza from friends and readers, but we had never managed to stop at this tiny, family owned operation in Kalaheo because at lunchtime we usually have very hungry—thus very cranky—children to bring home from the beach, and the thought of waiting with them while pizza baked was enough to make us lose our appetite. Several summers ago we hit upon a solution. On our way back from the beach, we called from a pay phone, ordered the pizza, and found it—miraculously—ready for us when our noisy crew arrived. We had only to cut-and-serve and temperaments improved as quickly as little mouths could chew-and-swallow.

The noise subsiding, we looked around and were pleasantly surprised by the extremely clean dining room and its cheerful red checked tablecloths. The walls feature murals of pizza serendipity —a pizza shaped like the island of Kauai, for example, with a "Garlic Grotto," a "Mushroom Valley," a "Grand Pizza Canyon," and a "Port Anchovy." Friendliness was in the air, from the waitress who smiled at each child and asked his or her name, to the sign inviting you to use the phone for local calls, but asking you to "limit calls to one minute."

But good as all this is, the pizza is even better, as fine as you'll find anywhere. The homemade dough—either white or whole wheat—is simply delicious, crunchy without being dry and with a fluted crust like a pie. You can even ask for garlic butter on the crust, which makes it shine, or in a dish on the side for dipping. The sauce pleased everyone, there was lots of cheese, and the Italian sausage was made right in the kitchen. Though pizza is expensive here as everywhere on Kauai, the portions are generous and quality unbeatable. A family size (15") starts at $11.95, but you may be tempted to try one of the outrageous special creations described on the menu, the "super" ($17.95), or one of the delicious looking sandwiches made on fresh baked rolls, bargain priced at $3-$4, or a salad. You can wash it all down with ice cold beer ($3.25 for 1/2 pitcher) or soda ($3.50/ pitcher). Success

made expansion inevitable, and a new Brick Oven has opened in the Kukui Grove Shopping Center in Lihue. Not as quaint as the Kalaheo Oven, the one at Kukui Grove is also not as hospitable to children, who have no spot where they can watch the dough spin into pizza during that hard, hungry time of waiting, especially at peak lunch and dinner times when the place is jammed.

If convenient, take the kids instead to Kalaheo. You'll find the roomiest and sturdiest high chairs on the island, and a smile and pleasant word for short persons no matter how cranky. When we left, our waitress gave each child a ball of dough (they had inquired about the origins of pizza) which obviously felt so good in the hands that it managed to say out of the hair—all the way home.

Rt 50 in Kalaheo. 11 am-11 pm daily. Closed Mondays. 332-8561. Kukui Grove Center branch open daily 11 am-11 pm. Closed Sundays after 4 pm. 245-1895.

Camp House Grill

Who would think to look for Kauai's best hamburger in the tiny town of Kalaheo (already sufficiently blessed, one would think, with the island's best pizza)? It's worth the drive to try a Camp House hamburger, a full 1/3 pound of ground chuck, served in a basket with a pile of some of the hottest, crispiest french fries you have ever tasted, and amazingly priced at $3.95.

If you were able to find Kalaheo, a tiny blip on the line of Rt 50 going west from Poipu, you would probably decide Camp House Grill looks too much like a greasy spoon, and drive right on by—that is, until you glanced at the parking lot—which is packed—or peeked in at the dining room—which is full. Once you're inside, you'll be pleasantly surprised by the crisp, clean decor: the woodgrain formica tables are well-spaced, the blue window frames a nice contrast with whitewashed walls, and even the green plants looking healthy and well-fed.

A cheerful waitress will seat you with a smile, no matter how much sand you bring in with you from the beach, or whether everyone in your party has managed to come up with an even number of shoes.

Though you cut some corners for such reasonable prices, paper placemats and napkins—even paper cups—are a small price to pay for such excellent food and pleasant service. And the placemats with a drawing of a sugar plantation 'camp house' give hungry kids an opportunity to color, crayons courtesy of management. Another generous touch: sodas are served in a "bottomless cup" for $1.25, and the drinks are served immediately and refilled cheerfully. Better yet, try a milk shake ($1.75), which you can see and hear being made fresh at the gleaming silver fountain machine. No soft ice cream made pasty with thickener, Camp House Grill's shake has the genuine texture of ice cream mixed with milk. Mikey knows: it looks just like the "soup" he always makes in the bowl when he has ice cream! Camp House Grill makes kids feel welcome. Ten-and-unders can eat a "menehune special" with a cheeseburger or a hot dog for only $2.25, while bigger little people can choose from junior burgers ($2.95 for 1/4 pound), fish, hot dogs, and four types of chicken breast sandwiches.

Everything is cooked to order, so you might have wait a bit, but it will all seem worth while once you start eating. Waimea burger ($4.50), otherwise known as a barbecue cheese burger, is perfectly cooked medium rare with tangy sauce and great cheese. In a Hanapepe Burger, broiled pineapple and teriyaki sauce make an ideal complement to the beef, swiss cheese, lettuce, and tomato. Onion rings ($2.75) would steal the show if it weren't already long gone with the french fries. Barbecue chicken ($4.25/half) is sizzling hot and spicy, as are the pork ribs. To cool it all off, you can have draft beer, available by the glass, or pitcher for $6.75.

Camp House Grill is clean, cheerful, and sincere. What you see is what you get—and then some extra. A deer head and a stuffed rooster look out through the window at what is passing by on Rt 560. Don't let that be you!

On Rt 560 in Kalaheo. 332-9755 for take-out orders.

Cantina Flamingo

As you turn the corner by the ocean, you may see a white volkswagon turned pickup truck, adorned with two pink flamingoes. This tells you not only to turn left, but hints at the serendipity of the restaurant. Housed in the downstairs of a comfortable old home, this restaurant has replaced an overpriced spaghetti house called the Aquarium. The aquarium is still there; the new owner had to promise to take care of the affable piranha when he took over!

Whatever the usual habits of piranhas, this is one of the friendliest restaurants on Kauai. Servers come to the table as if glad to see you, and they fill your needs promptly. As soon as you are seated, a huge plate of chips arrives, accompanied by delicious salsa with the color and taste of fresh preparation: tomato chunks, slices of green onion and cilantro leaves. Prices are just as welcoming. Just about everything on the menu costs less than $10, and dinner portions, served with rice and beans, are enormous. So are the margaritas, a house specialty, and you can choose from nine flavors, including such tropical delights as guava and coconut.

Mexican cuisine gets a new interpretation from the chef, who once presided over the kitchen at Plantation Gardens. He likes to cook with colorful, fresh vegetables, and so his Mexican creations make a personal statement. *Sopa de albundiga* ($2.25) was a delicious vegetable soup delicately flavored with cilantro and accented with spiced meatballs. Nachos ($4.75) come heaped over sauteed vegetables, including celery, onions, and peppers, as well as what you expect in the way of melted cheese, sour cream, and avocado. So if you usually put everything but the melted cheese on the side of your plate, be sure to tell the chef to double the cheese and hold everything else!

Entrees are generous, and some are more spicy than others. Cantina Relleno ($9.95), for example, is on the hot side: a flour tortilla stuffed with green chili peppers, chicken and cheeses, and topped with guacamole and sour cream. Milder, even somewhat bland, is the flautas Kauai ($9.95), a flour tortilla stuffed with chicken, shrimp, broccoli, and cheeses, and puff fried, garnished with tomatoes, sour cream, and guacamole. We found the best balance of flavor in the Flamingo's burrito, a flour tortilla generously stuffed with still-pink slices of tender, juicy steak; mixed with avocado, salsa, and a delicious green tomatillo sauce; and smothered in melted cheese. The food looks as wonderful as it tastes, with tostadas ($8.25) heaped in a spectacularly large crisp tortilla shell, and fajitas ($9.95) served with so much sizzle that you automatically look up to see where the smoke alarms are located.

You probably won't be able to finish everything, but waiters are helpful with carry-out containers, so you can plan on a lunch the following day. Those who like their enchiladas, tacos, and burritos cooked the old fashioned way can order from the a la carte menu, where items cost less than $5.00. The some who don't like it hot can choose a half-pound hamburger ($6.95) or a plain hunk of sirloin ($9.95). No matter your taste preference, be sure to save room for dessert. Deep fried macadamia nut ice cream ($3.25) "rolled in a blend of honey, cinnamon, and oats" (which the waiter told us with a grin was Team Flakes) is delicious, and the Mexican flan ($2.25) is outstanding, a caramel topped custard with a perfectly soft and creamy texture.

Cantina Flamingo fills an important need on the south shore: an inexpensive, high-quality family Mexican restaurant in a tourist area known for pricey dining. Children are treated with a smile and given glow-in-the-dark bracelets to play with as they wait for their food to be cooked. And with prices so reasonable, you can see why the restaurant is almost always full, even during the first three months of operation when it wasn't even listed in the Yellow Pages!

2301 Nalo Road in Poipu. Open daily 3:30-9:30 pm. Free nachos 3:30-5 pm. Coffee: $1.00. No reservations. 724-9505 for take out.

The House of Seafood

In the Poipu Kai Resort, the House of Seafood specializes in fresh fish, and because local fishermen are on good terms with the chef, you'll be able to choose from an amazing variety. This is a big advantage in winter months, when the surf can get too rough for the fishing boats. While other restaurants may have fresh fish in short supply and limited variety, the House of Seafood may be offering as many as eight or nine choices!

Most fish entrees are created by the chef as he contemplates what has been hooked that day and decides how best to cook it. You might find fresh sea bass cooked in parchment, fresh mahi mahi sauteed with macadamia nuts, fresh snappers of every hue, or even shark. Entrees are accompanied by clam chowder or salad, a vegetable, and delicious herbed wild rice. But you won't want to pass up the appetizers: mushrooms stuffed with crab ($3.95), or tangy deep fried artichokes ($3.95).

Attention to detail makes each part of the meal enjoyable. Bread sticks arrive with the first course, followed by rolls and butter with the entrees. The dinner salad is attractively served on a glass plate with croutons and radish, a better choice than the clam chowder which was thick rather than creamy. Service is polite and friendly, and you get the feeling that the staff is genuinely interested in doing the job well.

You can count on your fish to be generous and perfectly cooked, like fresh mahi mahi ($17.95) either flawlessly sauteed or baked in crust. Or try the more pungent fresh ehu ($17.95). On our most recent visit, we tried the opakapaka and onaga, both deliciously light, flaky, and very tender. As in most island restaurants, you might take the precaution of having sauces served on the side so that you can make up your own mind about whether they reveal—or obscure—the flavor of the fish. Entrees are usually accompanied with fresh vegetables carefully cooked and attractively served, like cauliflower served with a light and lemony cream sauce, although on our most recent visit, the stir-fry vegetables suffered from an overload of bean sprouts.

Your can spend a lovely evening in the comfortable, quiet dining room tastefully decorated with rattan and lots of leafy plants. Tables are well spaced for privacy and attractively set with green cloths and shining silver and glassware. On the well-selected wine list, you can find several good choices at reasonable prices, including a Geyser Peak Chardonnay for $17, and a Sterling Sauvignon Blank for $21. Our touchstone chardonnay, Edna Valley, was reasonably priced at $29.

At House of Seafood, the personal touch is everywhere. On one of the best children's menus on the island, children can choose from steak ($7.75), hamburger ($5.50), fresh fish ($6.75) and wait until you hear this entree from a generous and thoughtful management—grilled cheese ($3.95)! Each full dinner includes soup or salad, rice or french fries, vegetable, dessert and a drink!

Such recognition of children's real tastes is not surprising, for the chef has named his most special dessert after his own daughter. With great pride, your waiter will describe "Crepes

Tiffany," available only when the kiwi fruit is at perfect ripeness. Or you can try an excellent homebaked coconut strudel ($2.50) with lots of shredded coconut.

Come to the House of Seafood on a night with a moon. The dining room is open to the night air, and from the darkened room lit by the soft light of candles floating in bowls of flowers, you can watch the last light of evening fade, changing the pattern of darkness with each moment. Later as stars twinkle through thin filmy clouds, the full moon glows in the deep blue sky, while soft breezes rustle through the hibiscus leaves and crickets sing themselves to sleep.

In the Poipu Kai Resort. Credit Cards. Reservations 742-6433 (request a window table). Coffee $.95.

Keoki's Paradise

At Keoki's you might feel as if you've wandered onto the set of Gilligan's island. The tables are arranged on several levels around a wandering lagoon, where taro grows among the lava rocks, and you can even spot a frog or two resting among the lily pads. Green plants hang everywhere, and the night is filled with the sound of crickets. The wood tables are roomy and the rattan chairs comfortably upholstered. Ask to be seated outside, where dining is cooled by evening breezes and you can watch the light of evening fade and the sky turn luminous with shining stars. Should a passing shower threaten to douse your table, waiters will quickly raise the awnings!

One of the most successful restaurants on the south shore, Keoki's offers reasonable prices as well as the atmosphere of South Pacific chic. The long lines of hungry diners arriving at about 7 pm led to an expansion of the dining room, but even with the new space, you can expect lots of company when you arrive! The singles crowd hangs out at the elaborate bar, where you can order pu pus, nachos, and burgers. There is even a Seafood and Taco bar where you can sit and mix sashimi with chilis! Families like Keoki's too, particularly the extensive dinner menu, with several kinds of fresh fish, chicken, steak (sirloin only) as well as an enormous 26 ounce prime rib ($17.95 "while it lasts"). Meat prices being what they are, that has got to be about the best buy on

Kauai. Entrees include salad, rice, and fresh bread. Nine cost less than $10, and for about $6, children (and even adults) can choose a burger or chicken sandwich. Children's full dinners are reasonable, $4.50 for a hamburger or $7.95 for breast of chicken, inclucuding salad, bread, and rice.

Acting on the advice of the waiter, we did not order the fisherman's chowder ($1.95) and instead tried the dinner salad, which turned out to be a sharply seasoned Caesar salad with too much cheese, too many croutons, and the unmistakable limpness of bulk preparation. While the sourdough rolls seemed the brown and serve variety, the homemade bran muffins were excellent. The wine arrived well chilled, one of several reasonable choices on the list for under under $15.

The waiter recommended the fresh baked opakapaka ($18.95), which was moist, delicately flavored, and fragrant with basil. The fresh ahi ($15.95), however, was overcooked and dry, its flavor lost in the teriyaki sauce. The fresh ono ($16.95), was flaky enough but, on the small side, and served with a strongly flavored wine and caper sauce which should have been left on the side. The prime rib ($17.95), which was truly enough for two, was moist and tender though a bit weak on seasoning, but it proved once again that there's never been a bone too thick to chew. Tahitian shrimp ($13.95) turned out to be tender and deftly seasoned, and the lobster tail ($17.95) was moist and tasty, though be sure to tell the kitchen to hold the paprika, for someone in there just loves to use that red dust! The rice pilaf and vegetables, though, were excellent. Be sure to try the hula pie ($1.95), for which Keoki's is justly famous. The oreo crust holds macadamia nut ice cream topped with chocolate, whipped cream and macadamia nuts. Keoki's attracts a large clientele with reasonable prices and adequate cooking. Don't expect the kitchen to excel in subtle seasoning and you won't be disappointed. Simple dishes, like fresh fish plainly prepared, are the best. Keoki's is a good choice for the truly hungry, for it is hard to go wrong with 26 ounces of beef for $17.95, and for those who love the truly hokey, for you can giggle during dinner under those fake Polynesian torches about which Hollywood script you would most like to be acting out in Keoki's Paradise.

In the Kiahuna Shopping Village, Poipu. Credit cards.
Reservations a must 742-7534. House wines: Peter Francis white/ red or Robert Mondavi rose: $7.50. Coffee: $.75.
Dinner 5:30-10 pm. Seafood & Taco Bar 4:30-midnight.

The Koloa Broiler

The least expensive steak house on Kauai, the Koloa Broiler has devised a unique solution to the problem of overhead. Diners not only help themselves to salad, baked beans, and bread, but even cook their own entrees on an enormous indoor grill. A glass case at the entrance contains the menu in its raw form: mahi mahi ($7.95), barbecued chicken ($7.95), top sirloin ($8.95), beef kabob ($7.95), fresh fish ($9.95-$12.95) and a hamburger ($5.50). The waitress will bring your selection to you raw, recite a few cooking instructions, and then you're on your own, marking your cooking time by a huge clock positioned by the grill.

While this approach has obvious advantages, it is not foolproof. Hopping up and down to check the progress of your meal is hardly relaxing, and sometimes conversation distracts the attention you need for careful cooking. You end up being responsible for the quality of your dinner, so you can hardly send it back if it turns out raw or burnt. A few tips: you might try marinating your steak in the Italian salad dressing while you enjoy a cocktail. And despite instructions to the contrary, removing the foil wrapping from the chicken or fish in the final moments of cooking enhances the flavor. While your entree cooks, you can also toast some buttered bread.

The dining room is large and plain. Decorated with a few hanging plants and whirling ceiling fans, it has all the ambiance of a converted storeroom. And in certain spots, the fragrance of the grill is unmistakable. (This is one place where a non-smoking section is probably impossible!) But the real attraction here is unbeatable prices. It's a change of pace from the usual restaurant experience, and if you're on a tight budget, you won't find a more satisfying way to spend your evening or your money.

In the heart of Koloa. Reservations suggested 742-9122.
Credit cards. Children's dinner: hamburger or cheeseburger. Open for lunch and dinner, with a full bar.

Mangos

In the heart of old Koloa Town, Mangos took over the former quarters of the Koloa Fish and Chowder House, which failed in part because few people saw the reason to come to a cramped, dark and uncomfortable dining room located in the middle of a shopping center with no view. Remodeling was a big help, and even better was Mangos' new menu emphasizing a dining concept unique on Kauai: "Tropical Health" selections like cleanly broiled fresh fish, fresh fruit and vegetable salads, and oriental-type stir fry dishes. But because the owner hedged his bets with typical restaurant fare, the result was a menu with 30 selections for lunch and 49 at dinner!

Clearly not a low-maintenance menu! Something had to go, but what went was the special tropical health food emphasis. In fact, now you'll find just the reverse: chicken, fish, and shrimp dishes which are deep fried; mega-cholesterol beef cuts like prime rib and sirloin steak ($11.95-16.25) and high calorie items like ginger pork served with sweet plum sauce. The only nod we could find to the original health food concept was the "vegetable garnish" of crispy, uncooked broccoli and cauliflower which came with the entrees. As for plainly grilled fresh fish, our ono filet arrived with a pasty looking, very sharp wine sauce, which we were grateful to have asked for in a separate dish. The fish, however, should have been cooked on a cleaner grill. The rice and salad were nothing special, though the rolls truly were—light, warm and tasty.

Wine choices, though limited, are reasonably priced, with a Soave Bolla for $11 (less than the carafe of William Wycliffe, overpriced at $12) and a 1986 Robert Mondavi Fume Blanc for $19. Service is friendly and efficient.

In making its menu like other steak and seafood restaurants, Mangos has lost its opportunity for a special identity. Management will have to come up with a more distinctive cuisine to survive competition with restaurants in more desirable Poipu locations.

In Koloa town. Open lunch and dinner 11 am-10 pm. Credit cards. Coffee: $1.25.

Naniwa

The Japanese restaurant in the Sheraton Poipu Hotel, Naniwa won't whisk you away to an exotic world. The cuisine may be Japanese, but the restaurant was clearly designed with western clientele in mind, so you won't have to remove your shoes upon entering, and you won't be sitting on the floor.

Naniwa serves some of the finest Japanese cuisine on the island. Try red miso soup ($2.50), a wonderfully delicate broth garnished with tiny mushrooms and bean curd, elegantly served in a covered bowl with green onions nestled in the top. Spectacular! So is the sukiyaki, a magnificent platter of thin sliced beef, enoki and shiitake mushrooms, napa cabbage, bean curd, onions, noodles, watercress, and carrots. Not only beautiful to look at, this dish is beautifully prepared at your table: the beef tender, the vegetables fresh and crisp, the sauce tasty and the total combination a wonderful balance of flavors.

Tableside cooking is expensive, about $20 per person, and a minimum of two must order the same dish. Besides sukiyaki, you can choose yosenabe (seafood and vegetables) shabu shabu (beef) and uldonsuki (seafood). If you can't agree to share, you can choose from three full-course Japanese dinners ($21.50 to $23.95) or a reasonable variety of entrees including tempura ($15.95), fresh fish ($17.95), eel teriyaki ($19.25), teriyaki N.Y. steak ($18.95) and lobster ($28.50). Those looking for a more reasonably priced meal can try sushi, available in beautiful arrays ($13.25 and up) or by the piece.

Naniwa's chef makes the dining experience worthwhile, though you may find dining noisier that you'd like in a room which, though attractive, is rather small and crowded. Some necessary changes in staffing have made service much more efficient than when the restaurant opened last year. But other details still need work. While the meals are elegantly presented and attractively arranged, for example, you will eat them on paper placemats with disposable chopsticks. And though the restaurant overlooks a lovely garden and lagoon, the windows are not open to evening breezes. Most disappointing of all, the wine list is small and so undistinguished that the carafe of Robert Mondavi table wine may seem the best!

But after all, it's what is on the table that counts. At Naniwa, what's comes to the table is worth the wait and the noise.

In the Sheraton Poipu Beach Hotel. Reservations a must; specify a window table, as they are slightly more private . Coffee: $1.50.

Plantation Gardens

Set in several beautifully landscaped acres of specimen cactus and tropical flowers, Plantation Gardens is one of the most lovely and romantic restaurants on Kauai. The dining room and bar were originally the porches of a graceful old home, with soft evening breezes as delightful as the view, and you feel poised on the edge of the garden, with the mysterious shapes of the plantings dark against the star filled sky. Tables are spacious, with glasses and silver shining amid softly glowing candles and fresh flowers. Chairs are comfortable, and service is friendly, quiet, and leisurely, so that you can linger a long time over dinner and conversation.

Over the years, the quality of our dining experience at Plantation Gardens has gone up and down as chefs, managers and owners have come and gone. In fact, during summer, 1988, the kitchen was between chefs, a situation you could readily tell by the patchwork quality of the meal! The new chef has now arrived, or rather, one of the first chefs has returned to the kitchen after nearly ten years away from the island. Patrons who remember that far back will recognize his deft hand with seafood. You will probably find, in addition to the usual ahi and ono, at least one other variety such as uku, albacore, ulua, broadbill, or kahala.

On our most recent visit, the ahi ($17.95) was superb, cleanly broiled so that it was perfectly moist and tender, with a flavor so wonderful that it seemed a shame to use the teriyaki sauce at all. The fresh sauteed uku ($18.95) was moist and flaky, served with a sweet, fruity sauce that was a nice counterpart, although once again, the fish was even more delicious by itself. Entrees come with a tasty rice pilaf as well as a vegetable, in our case carrots with honey and tarragon.

The menu is also new. Prices are up, and you get less for your money. Salad is now a la carte ($1.95/medium $3.95/large), and for the extra charge it's a pretty monochromatic affair. With salad, your dinner is going to cost close to $20, although you still have a less expensive alternative, five 'lite cafe suppers,'such as a chicken breast teriyaki ($10.95) or a prime rib sandwich ($11.95), including vegetable and bread. Light suppers are served in the less formal patio adjacent to the cocktail lounge, as well as in the dining room. The wine list still contains some good choices at reasonable prices. Half the California whites cost less than $20, and a Sterling Sauvignon Blanc was fairly priced at $21.50. Ours arrived not quite chilled, so order early and request an ice bucket!

Dinner at Plantation Garden is going to be expensive, but you will probably remember the evening with pleasure, for the enchantment of the setting and the politeness of the service. Bring your camera for spectacular garden pictures before dinner, enjoy a lovely, relaxing meal, and walk through the Kiahuna's beautiful grounds afterwards.

In the Kiahuna Resort, Poipu. Reserve a day or two in advance 742-1695. Specify a window table but be prepared to wait for it—as much as 20 minutes if the staff is not efficient! Credit cards. Children's dinner $7.95 (prime rib, chicken, fish). House wine: Robert Mondavi $6.50/$12.00. Coffee/brewed decaf $1.50.

Tamarind, the Waiohai Hotel

The first luxury, gourmet restaurant on Kauai, Tamarind remains, on the whole, the most consistent in quality of food and service. The dining room is lovely, both formal and elegant, though you'll find no windows to let in fragrant evening breezes or offer glimpses of starry skies. Instead, the eye is drawn to the appointments of the room itself, the tables dressed in white linen, set with green and white china, shining glassware and a single bloom in a silver vase. Air-conditioned and plush, the room is hushed by thick carpet and linen tablecloths. Virtually the only sound you hear is the tinkle of glassware and silver to the strains of a piano in the adjacent lounge. You could be in New York instead of Kauai.

A new chef and a new menu have added some excitement to the cuisine, along with some new dishes with an Oriental touch. Escargots ($8), for example, are served in a shining copper pot without the shells or garlic of provincial France; instead, you'll find a wonderfully light cream sauce with julienned vegetables and an elusive flavor of ginger. A splendidly smooth papaya bisque ($4.75) makes a spectacular appearance in a carved papaya, and although some may find it overly sweet for an appetizer, it turned out to be a wonderful complement to the escargots. Lobster ravioli ($7.50) is also superb, three large pasta pillows perfectly cooked *al dente*, puffed with the shellfish, and attractively presented in a tomato ragout with creamy herb butter. Smoked breast of duckling ($7) is perfectly crisp and exceedingly tasty, attractively served with red oak leaf lettuce and pineapple relish.

During our most recent visit, the new *prix fixe* menu featured a combination of lobster in papaya ginger sauce and a filet mignon in green peppercorn sauce, an entree which we have enjoyed on previous occasions. Instead, we decided to try some of the chef's new a la carte selections. On the advice of our waiter, we chose broiled ono, served with a black bean and ginger sauce, and accompanied by shrimp fried rice rolled in a thin crepe of egg and tied with a knotted green onion. Very lovely to look at, but the fish, which was perfectly prepared, was too delicate for such a strongly flavored sauce. A better complement, in our opinion, was the lime and macadamia nut sauce which came with the broiled opakapaka ($23.50), and the kitchen was obliging enough to whip up an extra serving at our request, while we left the black bean sauce in its dish. Another interesting concept, and a more successful blend of flavors, was the lobster, scallops, and fresh fish sauteed with ginger and lychee in a papaya butter sauce ($24.50) . The sliced filet of beef with walnuts, boursin cheese, and cabernet sauce ($26.75) was perfectly cooked and tasty.

Desserts are one of Tamarind's finest achievements. The chocolate souffle ($6) was perfectly light, with a deep and rich chocolate flavor. Also exceptional was the passion fruit flan ($3) in a flaky crust colorful with strawberry slices. With the bill come spectacular dark chocolate truffles.

Winner of the *Wine Spectator's* coveted award, Tamarind's wine list has more than two hundred selections, each printed with vintage as well as price, watched over with great care by sommelier Jeffrey Courson. California wine-lovers will find most of the best vintners from Napa, Sonoma, Mendocino, or Central Coast, while those who prefer European wines will find one of the best selections anywhere. You'll find a variety of choices in the medium price range, and Jeffrey knowledgable about the choices.

By the end of the evening you will come to know him, as well as the maitre de and your waiter by their first names. The staff is attentive without hovering, and unfailingly pleasant. Each course is elaborately presented on china with silver domes topped with carved pineapples, and as each plate is removed, you are asked how you enjoyed what was on it. Every effort is made to make you —and not just your meal—the center of attention. From beginning to end, the dining experience is marked by an almost flawless attention to detail and by the chef's considerable expertise. As one of four island gourmet restaurants now featuring fine continental cuisine, Tamarind offers consistently fine food, professional service, and relatively speaking, fair prices. Two can expect to pay between $80 and $100 (less than at the Masters, Westin Kauai), and the evening will be so enjoyable that you will probably consider the money well spent.

In Poipu. 742-9511 for reservations, at least a day in advance.

Waiohai Sunday Champagne Brunch

A less expensive way to enjoy the talents of the kitchen is the Sunday Brunch, justly famous among local people as a truly magnificent feed. No ordinary affair of warmed over eggs and sausage, this buffet features five tables laden with a baroque display of meats, seafood, salads, fruits and pastries of every description. Each platter delights the eye with a colorful pattern of food ingeniously carved, sliced, sculptured, garnished, twisted even disguised as flowers or birds. You will find sashimi, not only ahi but whole ehu (red snapper), sliced in intricate criss-cross pattern from head to tail as well as octopus and shrimp (still in the shell), terrines and pates, salads and fresh vegetables, fruits and juices, croissants, cheese cakes, and pies of every flavor. Waffles come with whipped medallions of strawberry or banana butter. Before your eyes you can have an omelette created with your choice of fillings, a pasta tossed with marinara or cream sauce, or juicy roast beef sliced to your plate by a smiling attendant. As the morning wanes, the food selection changes, so even if your appetite flags under all this exercise, you might be tempted by some new confection just whisked out from the kitchen.

Even in this culinary Eden, however, there is a snake—in this case the winding line you must wait on for at least a half hour no matter when you join it. The line begins to form at 9 am. Since the dining room fills rapidly when the doors open at 10 am, arriving at line's end after 9:30 will probably condemn you to waiting until some of the first sitting retire from the field. That can take an hour, so arrive early, bring the paper, and enjoy some complimentary coffee while you make the acquaintance of those around you on line. The hostess suggests a 1:30 pm arrival for the shortest wait. The best solution: find friends to make a party of ten (that earns you a reservation) and call two days in advance. Just keep your fingers crossed as you walk past the line of hungry people not-so-patiently waiting their turn. ($21.50)

Eastern Shore Restaurants

Al and Don's

There used to be a sign outside boasting 25 breakfast selections. Now it's gone, but no matter. The food never was very good anyway, and the real attraction at Al and Don's is the view. From roomy booths next to enormous windows, you can see the ocean, rimmed with ironwoods, stretching out to the horizon. The decor, though nondescript, is pleasant, and the tables are large and comfortable. Waitresses bring coffee immediately, and your order is prepared quickly and served cheerfully. Food is reasonably priced though not memorable. The pancakes are a trifle heavy, and the corned beef hash, mediocre. The eggs are the best bet.

We had visited Al and Don's only for breakfast, when we could enjoy the restaurant's best attraction—the view! But as an experiment, we sent the four short people for a special outing, a private dinner with the babysitter. The results were, in a word, mixed. Only one of our four actually ate what was served, and their observations had the compassion and tact one would expect at their ages: the chicken cutlet was like rubber; the chicken stir fry was cold and mushy; the mashed potatoes were sticky; and jello was the best part of the meal. Their parting recommendation (which might well have been reciprocated by management, judging from our oldest child's description of the deportment of our youngest) was "Don't come back." On the other hand, prices are reasonable and, if you time your dinner carefully for before sunset—you might have better luck!

In the Kauai Sands Hotel, at the southern end of the Coconut Plantation Marketplace, Wailua. Credit cards. 822-4951. Open 7 am-10 am, and 6 pm-8:45 pm daily.

Barbecue Inn

With a comfortable, attractive, air-conditioned dining room, Barbecue Inn offers one of the best food values on the island. And it's the rare kind of place which will offer something special to just about everyone in the family. Grown-ups will love the shrimp tempura and teriyaki steak combination plate. The tempura is light, crispy and delicate, and the teriyaki steak skewers very tender and tasty. Accompanied by appetizer, soup or salad, homemade bread, vegetable, dessert, and a beverage, this is a real steal for under $10.

Kids will love the cheeseburger ($2.50), which you have to order off the lunch menu even at dinner. Bacon costs 75 cents extra, but it's a small price to pay for a burger which arrives still sizzling on a toasted sesame bun smothered with melted cheese and garnished with fresh, local manoa lettuce! On the dinner menu, those who can do without the bun can order the full hamburger steak dinner ($4.95). Another favorite is the teriyaki steak, a good-sized, tender rib-eye with perfectly flavored homemade sauce. Fussy eaters can choose from an enormous menu of 25 dinners—spaghetti, seafood platter, T-bone steak, prime rib—almost all at less than $8. Stick to the basics! Dishes like breaded chicken breast stuffed with crab ($7.95) may be disappointingly overseasoned. If you can't make up your mind, try the fried chicken platter, great for kids.

You will be surprised at the high quality of the "extras" which many restaurants pay scant attention to. Bread is homemade—light, fragrant, and exceptionally tasty. Your plastic basket will also contain some homemade "lavosh" which is buttery, almost like shortbread. It's so good, you will want seconds, so splurge on an extra order for only 60 cents. The fruit cup appetizer is all fresh—

pineapple, papaya, watermelon, honeydew, and mango—and so wonderful that you'll hope your kids will refuse to eat theirs because there are no canned peaches! The green salad would win no awards for imagination, but you'd be surprised at how much fun the kids have picking out the shredded cabbage and homemade croutons! And everyone will devour the homemade pies—coconut, chocolate, or chocolate cream—pies so light they are almost as amazing as the price: 75 cents a slice, the same as a Coke!

You will see a lot of working people coming off the job, and the portions are so enormous you can understand why. Waitresses are unfailingly cheerful, even when small children decorate the floor with crumbs and ice cubes. All this makes Barbecue Inn a good dinner choice for hearty eaters and hungry families, for anyone who appreciates ordinary food cooked extraordinarily well, as well as some very special treats.

In Lihue. 2982 Kress St (off Rice St). Closed Sundays. Dinner 4:40 pm-8:45 pm. Coffee: $.75. No credit cards. 245-2921.

The Bull Shed

The Bull Shed is famous for its prime rib—a thick slice of tender beef with a tasty bone (if you ask for it) and delicious, fresh horseradish sauce—still reasonably priced at $15.95, though prices have been creeping up dollar by dollar over the past year. Unfortunately, the Bull Shed is also famous for the difficulty of getting to the table in time to enjoy the famous ribs before the kitchen runs out, as it did during two recent visits. The problem wasn't late arriving diners; everyone was there before 7:30. The problem is waiting once you arrive, because of the no-reservations policy. And don't look for sympathy from the staff—they're used to people waiting around and looking unhappy.

We have tried hard to beat the system. We have done our best, despite cranky kids and frazzled babysitters, to arrive before 7 pm. On one visit, we even collected six friends to qualify for a reservation, but still ended up waiting 45 minutes, after refusing to accept two tables for two pushed together. And once your wait is over, you may find, as we did, that the prime ribs are all gone and what's left is pretty uneven. The broiled fresh ono ($14.95), which can be among the best, has also been overcooked and full of bones. The prawns and scallops ($13.95) have on occasions been too sharply seasoned. Of two racks of lamb ($14.95) ordered on the same night, one was tender, juicy, and delicious with teriyaki marinade, while the other was fatty and overdone.

A glance at the menu will tell you why the Bull Shed remains so popular. Entrees come with rice and the salad bar, and half cost less than $13. The wine list is also reasonable, with almost half the selections less than $15, including a Mirassou Monterey Riesling at $10.95. If you like white wine, order it right away because your bottle might need time to chill, as we have found on more than one occasion.

The dining room has been redecorated (the third time that the bar has been moved since we began our visits!) The result is more spacious dining, and more tables, though some are pretty small, particularly the triangular tables for two right by the ocean. Captains chairs are so close together that once you're seated in an inside chair, you can forget about getting out without asking everyone around you to move! It's a good thing that bread is no longer a serve-yourself affair but arrives at the table in a basket, and that dinner, according to the menu, includes "*a*" visit to the salad bar!

When we took the family, all our children ate everything that was served to them—a rare achievement. Lauren's teriyaki chicken breast was ($9.95) perfectly soft and juicy. Mikey was thrilled with his teriyaki sirloin ($12.95) , and Jeremy loved his rack of lamb ($14.95). Each made the most of the single visit to the salad bar.

After such satisfying dinners, you can almost forgive the Bull Shed for service that ranges from indifferent to inept. The setting is spectacular, just a few feet from the edge of a seawall, and from tables by the windows you can watch the waves roll towards the wall and crash in torrents of spray. On nights when the moon is full, the waves send gleaming ripples through the darkness. The best table in the house is located in a glass enclosed corner.

During a storm, the waves splash against the glass, and you may feel as if each forkful is going to be your last! If the evening is warm, be sure to request a table by a window which opens (not all do), for breezes in this restaurant are hard to come by. But then, by the time you get seated, the kitchen may be out of everything but coffee!

In Kapa'a on Rt 56. No Reservations. 822-3791. Credit Cards. Look for the sign (it's small) opposite McDonald's just north of the Coconut Plantation Marketplace, and turn towards the water. House wine: Inglenook ($6.95/3.95).

Casa Italiana

Would you expect to find superb pasta on a small tropical island in the Pacific, of all places? Casa Italiana will surprise you with wonderful noodles of every shape, color and size, fifteen different varieties! No matter which you try, linguini or fettucini, tortellini or spaghetti, at Casa Italiana, pasta is truly special, a homemade creation of love as well as skill.

The fettucini alfredo is as fine as you will find anywhere, the noodles perfectly tender and the cream sauce so delicate and understated that you can taste the pasta too. Or try cappeletti, the hat-shaped pastas filled with veal. A perfect complement is the linguini, with a more robust marinara sauce chunky with fresh tomatoes, sauteed mushrooms and green onion. Tortellini alfredo is very delicate, with a touch of nutmeg. In these dishes, the pasta is a separate taste and texture from the sauce, rather than simply something to wrap around your fork. The cheese is authentic, fragrant, fresh-grated romano and parmesan.

The owners clearly love what they do, and they are generous to guests. For example, instead of the spaghetti which comes with veal and chicken entrees, you can substitute one of the sumptuous pasta cousins and have it served as an appetizer for a modest $2 charge. The chef prides himself on his veal, and justly so, for the veal dishes are deftly cooked and flavorful. The veal scallopini al marsala ($15.95) is both tender and tasty. The veal parmigiana with tomato and wine sauce ($15.95) is moist and cheesy. Dinners include homemade pepper bread or garlic bread and also the salad bar, an attractive array of fresh vegetables and fruits with several tasty homemade dressings. In fact, you could make a delicious, inexpensive meal of pasta and salad bar ($1.95 extra with pasta entrees) alone. Although your choices on the wine list are limited —it comes down to Italian or Robert Mondavi—many are priced below $15.

You can enjoy this wonderful pasta in a comfortable dining room furnished attractively like a patio, with red tile floor, white patio chairs, marble topped tables set with red glasses and napkins. Hanging plants and a mural accent the red and white decor. Of the two dining rooms, the lower one, open to evening breezes on two sides, is more comfortable. The upper room, however, is also pleasant and available for private parties. Service is extremely friendly and efficient, and two can enjoy a delicious dinner for a reasonable price. If you have a yen for Italian food after all those papayas and mangoes, you couldn't make a better choice!

2989 Haleko Rd, Lihue (behind Eggbert's). Reservations 245-9586. Children's pasta dinners 40% off. House wine: C.K.Mondavi $4.95/$6.95. Coffee/brewed decaffinated $1.00. Dinner 5:30-10 pm daily. Credit cards.

Club Jetty

Overlooking Nawiliwili harbor, Club Jetty has two distinct personalities, which have about as much in common as Dr. Jeckyl and Mr. Hyde! Between 5:30 and 9 pm it is a family restaurant, but at 9 pm the highchairs are folded and the Club turns into a hard rock haven with lots of dancing and drinking. If you get in early with the family set, you are treated to moderately tasty Cantonese food at reasonable prices, as well as the very best chi chi on Kauai! Try the sweet and sour pork ($5.50) or the chicken black mushroom ($5.95). Although a bit expensive at $4, the spring rolls were an enormous hit with our children—crisp and fat and stuffed with crunchy vegetables. A less expensive version of stuffed crisp noodles, the crisp gau gee ($2.70), was almost as popular. We could choose our own vegetables to be stir fried — delicious! The menu also features several inexpensive American dinners.

Club Jetty's greatest appeal is its family-style friendliness. At 82, Mama still does most of the cooking, which the regulars who come for dinner missed when the Club was closed for a recent renovation, and also for Mama's cornea transplant! Now she's back in the kitchen, assisted by family members. Grandaughter Leinani is particularly friendly and helpful to guests trying to decide what to order. While dinner is being prepared, she takes restless youngsters to feed the fish just outside the window, helping little hands take aim so that the pieces of bead make it to the water. Leinani has the gift of making each child feel special, and she makes a "Banana Mana" fruit smoothie that puts a Shirley Temple to shame! And the dining room makes you feel at home as you look out over the harbor, where boats rock gently as the setting sun casts golden light on the mountains.

In Nawiliwili. Reservations suggested 245-4970. Credit cards. Closed Sundays. Free shuttle in Lihue area.

Dani's

At Dani's, you won't find an orchid on your plate, but if you order eggs, what you will find will be hot, tasty, and filling. Toast and kona coffee come free with breakfast, and you can choose from eggs, omelettes, pancakes, and Hawaiian dishes. The ham and cheese omelette is very cheesy and stuffed with ham, though the hotcakes are on the heavy side. Papaya pancakes intrigued us, until we discovered they were an uncommon item for good reason, a soggy consistency. The menu also offers a wide variety of sandwiches and hamburgers as well as lunch plates with salad, and an inexpensive New York steak. Full dinners start at $4.50 and include soup or salad, roll, rice, and coffee or tea.

With prices this low, expect to sacrifice atmosphere. The color scheme is woodgrain formica accented by florescent lights, but on the other hand, the large, modern dining room is bright, clean, and comfortably air-conditioned. Service is swift and efficient, and the hours are convenient for everything but late afternoon snacks and middle of the night cravings.

On Rice St in Lihue, across from Pay 'n Save. Breakfast 5 am-11 am. Lunch 11 am-2 pm. Dinner 5:30-9:30 pm. Sunday hours 6 am-11 am. 245-4991. Coffee $.40. Credit cards.

Dragon Inn

Perched on the second floor of a small shopping center on Rt 56 near Kapa'a, Dragon Inn looks big, bright, and cheerful. Inside, the dining room is clean, if sparsely furnished. The decor may be no more than the sum of woodgrain formica tables, green leafy plants, and a red carpet, but the windows frame beautiful Sleeping Giant mountain, the tables are not overly close together, and the food is terrific!

This is a first-rate family restaurant. Waiters are very tolerant of the inevitable whining amid the dining. After listening with a smile to our kids describe what they would refuse to eat if he brought it to the table, our waiter politely revised their orders as they worked out the final details of who would share what with whom. He seemed to know that once he got the egg rolls on the table, the cranky crew would settle down, their behavior following that timeless rule: you can't chew and complain at the same time. And he was right. After superb egg rolls ($3.50 for 3), fried won tons and gau gee ($2.50 each), the main courses proved as generous as the prices are reasonable. As the kids got down to the work of dividing up everything into metrically equal portions, we adults recognized that we had passed that magical point when everyone's plate has something on it and you know the rest of the meal is coasting.

Silver Flower Scallop soup ($4.95) was delicious, tasty and piping hot, more popular with the children than chicken and corn soup ($4.50) which had "things" in it. The beef and broccoli ($4.75) was so tasty that the short people clamored for a second order. Chicken with bamboo shoots and vegetables ($4.75) was full of tender and delicious chicken. Cake noodle was crispy and tasty, and served with generous chunks of meat. The shrimp canton ($4.75), with eight juicy shrimp, was a perfect balance of sweet and sour. And when seven can feast for $73 including tip, that's a good deal as well as a good meal.

We saw lots of families, some with three generations, and several high chairs, but in this restaurant booster chairs are made by stacking two dinner chairs—an idea which might have worked, but whose time had clearly not yet come for our youngest. She sat on her knees instead and had a great time dropping rice, grain by grain, onto the floor.

There is no wine list to speak of, but you can order chardonnay, cabernet, and white zinfandel by the carafe, as well as Chinese beer and all the tea you can hold. Come early for dinner; by the time we left at 7:45, the place was packed! If you try Dragon Inn lunch, you can order an unbeatably priced lunch special with soup and a choice of 12 entrees for only $3.95.

In the Waipouli Plaza, on Rt 56 in Wailua. Reservations 822-3788. Take out menu. Lunch 11 am - 2 pm. Dinner 4:30 pm - 9:30 pm. Closed Sunday and Monday. House wine: C.K. Mondavi: $12.

The Eggbert's

Eggbert's dining room is spacious, bright with sunlight, and comfortable. Even better, the kitchen can serve among the finest omelettes on the island, though on our most recent visit we found prices up while service remained as slow as ever. If you like omelettes, you can choose from 11 varieties, including sour cream and chives ($3.95), fresh mushroom ($3.55), and the "vegetarian delight" ($5.45) which is so stuffed you can hardly get your mouth around it, but be sure to ask the kitchen to hold the onions unless you love them sharp! Larger, 3-egg omelettes are also available for more money (not to mention cholesterol).

No matter the egg count, omelettes are accompanied by rice or hash brown potatoes or toast. Separately priced additions allow you to transform the basic 2-egg omelette ($2.45) into your own creation, and if your omelette comes out on the dry side, be sure to complain, and the staff will cheerfully bring another one. The breakfast menu also features eggs benedict ($5.95), delicious banana pancakes ($2.95), and a before 7 am special ($2.95). Children can choose pancakes ($1.15), pig in a blanket ($1.50), or an egg plate ($1.20 and up). Coffee is $.75 and is brought immediately. Service is on the poky side, so families might want to order some a la carte toast right away.

4483 Rice St in Lihue. Reservations unnecessary. Credit cards. 7 am-3 pm daily. Call for weekly dinner schedule. Coffee $.75.

Hamura Saimin Stand

According to rumor, Oahu businessmen have flown to Kauai just to have lunch at Hamura Saimin. To look at the weather-beaten exterior, you'd have your doubts. The tiny building encloses—just barely—twin rectangular counters with stools. A recent facelift has made the room look cleaner and more like a luncheonette, but now that the kitchen has been moved out of the center and into the back, you can no longer have a ring-side seat to watch the cook stir and chop and make things sizzle. The inevitability of change, yes, though some traditions die hard. The sign still warns: "No Gum Under the Counter." This year, our kids were old enough to check!

On this counter is served some of the finest saimin around, and you come to want to believe the rumor about the Oahu businessmen and their expense account lunches. Airfare could certainly be offset with bargain food prices: for $2.30 you get the saimin special—tasty and fragrant soup with noodles, chock full of vegetables and meats. The perfectly flavored won ton soup or won ton min is only $2.60. To take the saimin out costs .30 extra for the container, but it's worth it to escape the cramped little room and head for the beach. Barbecued beef or chicken sticks at $.75 are another find, tasty, moist, and perfectly spiced. Light homemade *manapu* (a sweet cousin of the pretzel) is a great dessert for kids, while adults can try the lilikoi chiffon pie ($.95).

There's not much variety, but what the cook cooks is very good indeed, and the visit is like a trip into the island's past, a time before tourism brought butcherblock tables and bentwood chairs, air-conditioning and gourmet teas—a time when sticking gum under the counter, though frowned upon, was still possible. So throw away your Bubble Yum before going inside, and try this taste of authentic Kauai!

2956 Kress St, Lihue. Cash only. 245-3271.

Hanama'ulu Restaurant & Tea House

You could not select a better place to share a really special evening with friends than the Tea House, because this restaurant combines delicious food with the friendliest service on the island, and, as if that weren't enough, a Japanese garden setting to make everything seem just a bit magical. Here you can dine on soft mats at low tables next to the goldfish and water lilies. Children can wander around and count the carp (tell them to be careful; one of our two-year-olds tumbled in!). Local families have been coming to the Tea House for more than sixty-five years, when it was the only dining establishment on the only road on the eastern shore! Today they still appreciate superb cooking at reasonable prices, and it's a rare wedding, anniversary, welcome or farewell party that does not take place in one of the tea rooms by the garden. So reserve your tea room several days in advance!

The Miyake family cooks with subtlety and flair, and creates a genuinely special cuisine, with 35 Chinese and Japanese entrees at reasonable prices from $3.25-$13.50. We recommend the won ton soup ($4) as the finest anywhere, generously garnished with scallions, pork, and slices of egg foo young. Children will love the crispy fried chicken with its delicate touch of ginger ($4.75); the boneless pieces are just the right size for little hands. Also try crispy fried shrimp ($7.50) and teriyaki beef skewers ($5.75).

When our party is large enough, we ask the owner to order a several course dinner. And we are always delighted with the new dishes we discover. The lobster with special butter is superb — exceedingly tender and subtly flavored. Shrimp tempura ($8) is spectacular, served on an enormous, beautiful platter, and the taste is just as wonderful. The sashimi is fresh and beautifully arranged, the slices of ahi and ono both slender and fragrant. A specialty,

mushrooms stuffed with crab ($5), is lighter than many versions of the dish, and very tasty. In fact, each time we think we have discovered everything wonderful about this restaurant, we are surprised with a new creation, like crispy tofu tempura ($3.25) served with teriyaki sauce and green onions, and incredibly tasty deep fried scallops wrapped in bacon and served with asparagus.

If you would like to skewer your own vegetables, seafood, meat, and chicken, ask to be seated in a lovely room with table top broilers and a sushi bar, a self-contained Japanese restaurant and sushi bar. We prefer the tea room by the gardens, where we can listen to crickets sing the songs of evening while stars light up the velvet sky. If mosquitoes like to pick on you while ignoring your friends, don't be bashful about asking for a mosquito coil. The incense smell is great, and it keeps the bugs away. Over ten years of dining here, this special restaurant has never let us down. The cooking is consistently superb, the prices remarkably reasonable, the service exceptionally friendly, and children are treated with more than usual tolerance by waitresses like Sally and Arlene who genuinely love them. Because this is a restaurant where you should sample as many dishes as possible, and because it is such a special place, we like to save the Tea House for our last night with our Kauai friends, and ask any *kapunas* who might be listening to speed our return! You shouldn't miss the Tea House either.

Call Sally for reservations or to arrange special dinner menus at 245-2511. (You can even request our Underground Guide special dinner!) Credit cards. Full bar. House wine: Robert Mondavi $6/$10. Closed Mondays. Lunch 9 am-1:30 pm; Dinner 4:30 pm-9:30 pm. Banquet facilities available.

Inn on the Cliffs, Westin Kauai

As you can expect at the Westin, your meal is only the main course of your evening, which begins ceremoniously with a limousine ride to the hotel's boat dock, where a silver token ($2 deposit for non-hotel guests) allows you to board an elegant Venetian launch for a romantic journey across an enormous man-made lagoon, where fountains splash in shining arcs through statues of fanciful beasts and fish. At your destination, liveried attendants hand you from the craft to the walkway leading to Inn on the Cliffs.

The restaurant's elegant three-level design takes full advantage of its cliff-side perch on the edge of Kalapaki Bay. You enter at the middle level, and as you stand in the foyer, suspended between the lounge upstairs behind you and the dining level in front of you below, you look out to sea through giant windows. Open to all three stories, the dining room has the sense of great space and light, and yet despite its grand dimensions, which may remind you at once of a baronial castle or an art museum, the room has an almost contradictory feeling of intimacy. Each table, with its cluster of plushly upholstered chairs, seems to create its own separate space, and the Oriental carpets and fine works of art can make you feel as if you're dining in a private home. White linen cloths are set with gleaming china and silver, fresh orchids bloom in white seashells, and candles twinkle in brandy glasses. In the bar upstairs you'll even find a fireplace for damp rainy nights, with two couches just the right size for close encounters.

Dinner could not be more relaxing. Melodies from the piano and bass seem to rise, then float down to the lower levels. Through the giant windows, you can watch the waves roll slowly into the bay, crested with white foam and gleaming in the moonlight. Or, because the restaurant is also in the glide path for the airport, you can watch the jets, headlights ablaze in the night sky, fly past the restaurant's huge windows to bring the next load of lucky vacationers to the garden isle.

But the view and the restaurant, spectacular as they are, make up only part of Inn on the Cliffs's special charm. In a word, the seafood is wonderful, and you'll find a lot to choose from on the menu. In addition to jet-set clams, shrimps, lobster, and oysters, you'll find at least half a dozen local fresh fish entrees ($21-$24),

while those who prefer the turf to the surf can choose teriyaki chicken ($13) or a first-rate New York steak ($18), as well as pasta dishes available in either entree or appetizer portions ($16/$8).

The specialty of the house is the fresh fish, and it is truly special, served in generous portions which can be either broiled or pan fried. The fish is beautifully prepared and attractively served, crispy gold on the outside and yet meltingly tender, with the natural flavors enhanced simply with lemon and butter. Although Chef Clarence Nishi can whip up a delicious herb wine sauce on request, purists like ourselves who love the natural flavors undisguised will appreciate the kitchen's clean, crisp pan frying as the best way to taste the subtle flavors of onaga ($22), ono ($20), or mahi mahi ($24) and opakapaka ($23) which pleased a skeptical, first-time fish eater. The chef usually offers at least one special preparation each night, and the sea bass served with straw mushrooms, tofu, and beurre blanc sauce was firm and soft, with a texture like lobster.

You can choose from a wide array of appetizers, including some delicious fresh pasta entrees available in a half portion. Linguini and veal marsala ($9.25) is outstanding, as is the linguini ordered "low cholesterol" with only olive oil and garlic. Equally good are the broiled scallops ($8), perfectly tender and served with avocado and a delicious salsa with character. Also fine though not quite as special are sauteed ginger shrimp with cilantro and spring onions ($8.50), and duck salad with ravioli ($8.50). Soups are truly wonderful, both the spicy bouillabaise ($4.95) generous with fish and shellfish in a broth flavored with pernod and saffron, as well as the clam chowder ($3.50), delicately seasoned, creamy, and filled with clams and potatoes.

Entrees arrive with fresh vegetables, in our case sauteed snow peas, red peppers, and red potatoes garnished with dill. Mini baguettes of sweet french bread are warm and tasty, and you'll find some excellent light pastries for dessert, like a spectacular hazelnut and chocolate sponge cake. The wine list offers a wide selection of California 1985 and 1986 wines for less than $25, such as a 1986 Sterling Sauvignon Blanc for $23, as well as some good values for a little more, like a 1986 Sonoma Cutrer for $30. Service is efficient while still leisurely, and everything is arranged to be elegant and at the same time not overly formal.

The Inn on the Cliffs offers a winning combination: spectacular location, beautiful dining room, friendly service, and delicious fresh seafood. You can't ask for much more, even if prices are a bit higher than in other island seafood restaurants. If you are on a budget, you can choose a fresh fish entree and the clam chowder, skip dessert, and get away with about $25 per person. You can exchange your silver token for $2 credit on your dinner!

Or come for lunch, enjoy the boat trip in daylight, and find prices about a third less ($16-$20) for a 6 oz portion of fish. Whichever you choose, this is a restaurant you should not miss!

In the Westin Kauai. Reservations at least two days in advance, for two seatings, at 6 pm or 8 pm: 245-5050. Free valet parking.

Jacaranda Terrace, Kauai Hilton

Arranged on two levels, Jacaranda's attractive dining room looks out over the garden through glass doors that slide open to evening breezes. When weather is not so cooperative, the dining room is closed and comfortably air-conditioned. The upper tier is centered around a large table which offers moderately priced breakfast and dinner buffets. Along the rear wall, tables are recessed for privacy, and you can dine in what seems to be a small private room, tastefully decorated with wallpaper and prints. The result is quiet, relaxing, and very pleasant.

Because most hotel guests eat at this dining room, you can order almost anything—eggs, soup, sandwiches, salads, or hamburgers—at almost any time of day. At dinner, you can also select from 9 entrees served with potato or rice and vegetables. Prices vary widely, from a bowl of saimin ($5) to veal marsala ($16.50), with chicken, shrimp, steak and fish in between. The reasonably priced wine list has several good choices for less than $20.

We began our dinner with soup, a fresh baguette and butter. Though expensive for a small cup, the tomato soup ($3) was excellent—fresh, pungent with spices, and piping hot, while the cream of mahi mahi was rather pasty. Of the entrees, the roast prime ribs ($14.50) was the better choice, for it was a good-sized portion, tender, juicy and very tasty. The veal marsala would have been better without the thick and heavy sauce which pretty well obliterated the flavor of the veal. Both entrees were served with zucchini and carrots still crunchy and colorful. The baked potato was first rate, served with tiny dishes of sour cream, chives, and crisp bacon. Ordering from the menu seemed a better choice than the buffet, judging from the plates we saw carried by, heaped high with salad, fruit, and entrees with a lot of sauce.

Service is efficient, polite, and very friendly. Our waiter Ralph made the evening pleasurable with his genuine concern. When the cork disintegrated, the assistant manager whisked the wine bottle away and had a new one poured into iced glasses, properly chilled, within minutes. Capable staff like this can make a hotel restaurant into one you may remember even after you pay your bill and are on your way to the airport. If you order carefully, you probably won't have a bad dinner at Jacaranda, and the odds are good that you'll enjoy the evening.

In the Kauai Hilton. Reservations 245-1955. Credit Cards. Children's menu: half price of most selections. Coffee/brewed decaf $1.35 (decaf $1.50 at dinner).

Jimmy's Grill

Until a couple of years ago, a ramshackle building dozed on a dusty corner of main street, Kapa'a. The downstairs was home to a few dimly lit stores with wares probably just as well left in shadow, and a bar with the hapless name Ding's. Upstairs, the windows of empty apartments stared down like vacant eyes on the bewildering pace of modern day doings. Occasionally, the building came briefly to life—on hot fourth of Julys when sales of firecrackers turned brisk, or when local boxing matches drew the competitive and the curious. Now the weatherbeaten string of sleepy small businesses has been transformed into smart shops featuring upscale memorabilia, as well as a trendy new bar *cum* restaurant called Jimmy's Grill. The "Historic Hee Fat Building" has been reborn!

Jimmy's sign claims "Lunch Forever," and the decor tries to capture the carefree quality of endless waves and suntans. You enter Jimmy's through what used to be Ding's, only now the bar is a full two-story affair completely open to the street on the two sides of its corner location. Once inside, you'll find yourself on an indoor sand dune, improbably set with tables, chairs and an upholstered furnishing labeled "Party Couch." Behind the dune is a wide flight of stairs to the restaurant above, offering those who ascend an ever-changing perspective on a neon topless female winking from her perch on the rear wall. You will also pass by color photos and surfboards marked with the signatures, initials, and greetings of hundreds of happy campers.

The dining room, which takes up the whole top floor of Hee Fat, is pleasantly spacious. White walls and rafters are decorated with colorful surfboards and maritime flags, as well as an occasional pair of sneakers, and banks of green plants separate tables into clusters. Tables for two line the small balcony overlooking the main street of Kapa'a, and on the opposite wall are several roomy booths with bright red vinyl bench seats, the kind that will remind you of stationwagons called woodies. When breezes cooperate, the room is cooled by the cross ventilation, though the booths get some of the smoky smell from the grill, and the balcony gets the exhaust from street traffic. When temperatures climb on main street, however, remember what happens to hot air!

Lunch, says the sign, is forever, so the menu is the same throughout the day: burgers, sandwiches, munchies, as well as assorted entrees. We found the food competently prepared if uninspired. Hamburgers are reasonable in size and price (1/3 pound for $4.75), and moderately tasty. Shoestring fries seem to be prepared in large batches, since only one of our five servings was, in the words of our nine-year-old judge, "soft enough to chew." The others, probably from the previous batch, were cool and hard as potato sticks. The mahi mahi sandwich ($6.95) would have been better if the grill had been cleaner. Voted best by the children: the milk shakes ($2.25) and the waitress Bridget, one of the friendliest we have met, a paddling coach moonlighting during the local school's Christmas break.

You probably won't leave Jimmy's Grill disappointed. The food is adequate, and many people like the friendly openness and laid-back informality. Except perhaps the ghost of Hee Fat, wandering back for one last bewildered glimpse as the sun sets over the mountains.

Main St, Kapaa. 822-7000. Credit cards.

Kapa'a Fish & Chowder House

One of the few seafood specialty restaurants on the eastern shore, the Kapa'a Fish and Chowder House has an attractive exterior decorated with fishing nets and nautical gear. A newly landscaped entrance has replaced the old parking lot, making the front dining area is much less noisy. But the "garden room" in the rear, a peaceful oasis filled with hanging ferns and plants, is the place you want to request when you make a reservation.

The specialty is fresh seafood, from both local and distant seas. You'll find San Francisco crab, New England bluepoint oysters and steamer clams, sea scallops and Ipswich clams, and shrimps of all kinds. In addition to more than a dozen seafood entrees, the menu offers chicken ($9.95), a 16 oz New York steak ($17.95) and 18 oz of prime rib ($17.95). Entrees include choice of french fries, pasta, rice pilaf or steamed rice, as well as a vegetable, corn fritters and pumpkin muffins. The wine list contains some creditable selections at reasonable prices, including a good value in a French table wine, Chateau St Jean, at only $12.50.

This is an ambitious menu, and probably not surprisingly, the kitchen performs unevenly. The Koloa Fish Chowder ($3), served attractively in a copper pot, has been overly thick and heavily flavored with thyme. The New England clam chowder is sometimes more balanced, although the flavor of both soups is much improved with the sherry, a $.50 option. During our visits, the fish has ranged from overcooked and dry to properly moist and tender. One thing has been consistent, however: stay away from the sauces and ask to have the fish broiled or plainly sauteed. Most recently, the ono filet ($14.95), which should have been sweet and delicate, was just about ruined by a heavy wine sauce with nuts and capers. And the onaga, which the waiter described as served with a lemon butter sauce, arrived with a thick white cream sauce which we, with some difficulty, scraped off. The ahi teriyaki ($15.95), on the other hand, was much better, a generous portion cleanly broiled and very tender, with a tasty marinade that enhanced rather than overwhelmed the flavor of the fish. With the entrees, you get a choice between pasta, which is rather garlicky, or rice, or crisp, hot french fries. The fresh steamed carrots were good though not exceptional.

Over the last few years, one thing has been consistent about the service: it is reliably uneven—usually well-meaning, but somewhat inept. On one visit, our waiter attempted to insert the corkscrew into the wine bottle without first removing the covering from the cork. More recently, our waiter brought the wrong wine and then, correcting that mistake, broke the cork while opening the right one. Later, when we told him that the thick white sauce we were trying to scrape off the onaga filet did not appear to be the "lemon butter" sauce he had described to us, he said it looked like lemon butter sauce to him!

Given the unevenness of the kitchen and serving staff, dining at the Kapa'a Fish and Chowder House means taking your chances. If you catch it right, you can enjoy a pleasant seafood dinner in the garden room, softly lit with lanterns and candles. But you'll spend nearly $20 for that dinner, which would cost you about a third less at the Wailua Marina, for example, where the ambiance may be less sophisticated but the cooking more reliable.

In northern Kapa'a on Rt 56. Credit cards. Dinner from 5:30 pm daily. Reservations 822-7488. Specify the garden room. House wine: Summit $8/$4. Coffee: $.90. 7 children's entrees half-price.

Kauai Chop Suey

Kauai Chop Suey combines unpretentious surroundings, superb cooking, and unbeatable prices. Three connecting dining rooms, usually crowded with local families, are clean, bright, and cheerful, with well-spaced tables and fly fans to keep the air moving. The decor is a crisp combination of red and white, accented with red Chinese lanterns and green leafy plants.

The real attraction is the prices. A big tureen of scallop soup ($4.95) was sensational, with a subtly seasoned light broth, tender slices of pork and scallops, and an egg-drop texture. The shrimp canton ($4.75) was a perfect balance of sweet and sour, and the shrimps, eight large ones, were still crisp from being deep fried and exceedingly tender. Special fried rice (at $5.75 the most expensive dish on the large menu) was indeed special—especially tasty, especially generous, and chock full of delicious roast pork, chicken, shrimp, black mushrooms and crunchy snow peas. In Kauai Chow Mein ($5.75), shrimp, chicken, steak, and char sieu are blended in a colorful combination with broccoli, cauliflower, and carrots.

Your level of satisfaction, we discovered, has a lot to do with the service, which has a lot to do with the work load in the kitchen. Even if you see empty tables, the owner may tell you to come back in 15 minutes, and in this way control the pace at which the three chefs have to cook. Once you are seated, you may not see your waitress for a while. That's because there is only one waitress, and she takes the orders from more than thirty tables in all three rooms! Two other waitresses serve the food and a couple of busboys clear the plates. It's not a very efficient system, and it certainly lacks the personal touch, but the prices are amazing, and you can bring along your own wine or beer to make the waiting more pleasant! Think twice, however, about bringing the kids—unless you feed them before you come! To bring food home will cost you 21 cents a box: you pay and you pack! Be warned: your feet must be across the threshold by 9 pm or you will be told, with great politeness, that the kitchen is closed.

In the Harbor Village Shopping Center, Lihue. No reservations. Take out 245-8790. Lunch 11-2 pm Tues through Sat. Dinner 4:30-9 pm Tues through Sun. No beer or wine, but tea is free.

Kiibo

Kiibo has a pleasant, though small dining room with a clean, though utilitarian decor. Comfortable upholstered chairs surround bamboo colored tables, and brown lattice adorns the white walls. Everything is understated, even the air-conditioning!

The menu is actually a photo album, in which traditional Japanese dishes are described with photographs. A wonderful feature, you can order tempura a la carte ($1/selection) and select from five different types of fresh fish, chicken, pork, beans, tofu, onion, sweet potato, carrots, even eggplant. Whatever you choose will be both light and crisp, each flavor unique and meltingly delicious. Even the parsley was crunchy and still green. The teriyaki ($5.50) was another success, sweet yet tangy and both juicy and tender. The sukiyaki ($6.50) arrived in a steaming iron caldron, rich and pungent with sauce and translucent noodles.

Priced from $4.75, dinners include miso soup, a bowl of rice and another of sauce, attractively displayed on a square tray. Combination dinners cost more, between $11 and $15. Lunch is a better deal, however, with selections from $3.85 and about a dollar less than the same choices on the dinner menu. Lunch is also the better meal; given the cautious size of the portions, dinner might leave you hungry! For pretty much the same prices, you could find a better quality dinner in more lovely surroundings— for example, at the Hanama'ulu Restaurant and Tea House, or Kintaro in Kapa'a.

2991 Umi St, Lihue. 245-2560. Cash only! Lunch daily 11 am-1:30 pm. Dinner daily 5:30 pm-9 pm. Closed Sundays. Children's dinners $5.

The King and I

The King and I is one of those wonderful restaurants you always dream of discovering tucked away in a shopping center, like your child's favorite toy under his socks in the corner of the closet. Well, The King and I really is a dream come true, not only for the diner, but also for the owners, a family who fled Cambodia by boat, settled in Hawaii and trained in Honolulu's famous Keo's restaurant, waiting and saving for the chance to open up on their own.

Surprisingly pleasant and comfortably air-conditioned, the dining room is as modest as the prices. White linen tablecloths are topped with glass in an attractive compromise between attractiveness and utility. A definite step above formica! On walls painted a warm and friendly shade of pink are large paintings of Siamese ladies and rural scenes. Orchids and palm leaves give the tables a tropical touch.

But the real attraction at The King and I is the food. For most people, each dish will be an adventure into unknown and exotic tastes. Don't be bashful! The menu is large enough to appeal to a variety of tastes. Everyone will love the spring rolls ($5.25) which are crisp and light and wonderfully tasty. Attractively arranged on a manoa lettuce, with mint leaf and cucumber, and served with a delicious peanut vinegar dipping sauce, the spring rolls are so special that some customers make a meal of several orders!

But it would be a mistake to miss the other dishes that come out of this extraordinary kitchen. Lemon grass soup ($6.95) is served piping hot, with wonderfully fragrant clouds of steam. Shrimps served with a peanut sauce are meltingly tender, attractively arranged with shredded cabbage and tomato wedges. Or try the fried rice flavored with tomato, cucumber, and cilantro and garnished with sliced water chestnuts. Don't pass up the fried Thai noodles, delicately light and heaped in a small mountain with sliced scallions and bean sprouts.

Ginger fish turned out to be fresh mahi mahi breaded and fried crisp, served in a mild sauce flavored with ginger and scallions. The curries are outstanding, and you can select from three. Yellow curry is flavored with saffron, and would be the easiest to identify as a "curry." The green curry takes its color—and flavor—from fresh basil. The red curry was the sweetest, flavored with coconut. Best of all, in our opinion, is a curry not on the menu, but the favorite of a Kauai friend—a mild, sweet curry, flavored with peanut and coconut and chock full of tender chicken. You can ask for it as Micki's Favorite curry ($5.50).

The basil and other spices are grown fresh in Kilauea, and even the coconut ice cream is especially rich in flavor because, out in the kitchen, vanilla ice cream is mixed with special Thai coconut milk. Or try Thai tapioca pudding, more soupy perhaps than the lumpy stuff you may remember from school lunches, and flavored with delicious apple-bananas and coconut. The wine list is modest in both size and price. Most wines cost below $20, as well as beers, including a Thai beer, Singha, in a large bottle for $2.75.

The King and I is unique on Kauai, the only restaurant serving Thai cuisine, and a great choice for those evenings when you find it hard to look at another ahi or ono. You'll love the change of pace, the distinctive cuisine, and the friendly family atmosphere. And when you get your bill, your royal pocketbook will hardly notice.

4-901 Kuhio Highway, Wailua. Reservations two days in advance: 822-1642.

Gaylord's at Kilohana

Kilohana, once the heart of a 1,700 acre sugar plantation, is a special place. Wandering through rooms which have the spacious beauty of large proportions and wide verandas, you can easily imagine the gracious pace of life before airplanes and traffic lights. With the mountains behind and rolling lawns all around, you can glimpse, even if briefly, a way of life now forever lost. Browsing the shops brings you quickly up to date: trendy clothes and jewelry, and in the Kilohana Gallery, a fine collection of work by artists from Kauai and the other Hawaiian islands.

Named for Gaylord Wilcox who built Kilohana, the restaurant is in the dining room and on the veranda, looking out over the manicured lawn and gardens lush with leafy ferns and brilliant tropical flowers. In the evening, the flagstone terrace is lit with lanterns, and rattan chairs surround comfortable tables decked with white linen and pink napkins arranged like fans. Gaylord's is one of the most romantic restaurants on Kauai, with the kind of setting you'd want to star in if your life were a black and white movie. Candles on the tables flicker softly in gentle breezes, and from your chair beneath the roof you can peek out at stars shining in the velvet sky. As you look out at the gardens lit by the moon and stars, you can feel the soft tropical breezes which rustle the leaves.Waiters in tuxedo shirts and cummerbunds move discreetly, anticipating your every desire.

If only romance were an entree on the menu! Unfortunately, the food at Gaylord's has not yet developed an identity as special as the setting. Entrees are expensive, and unless you come for "light supper" (5 to 6:30 pm) your least expensive dinner choice is prime rib, at $17.95.

More than once, we have found appetizers to be the best course. The duck breast salad ($4.95), for example, is consistently excellent, the duck lean and crispy, and the raspberry sauce both sweet and tart. The grilled duck breast ($5.95) is also first rate. With your entree you can choose a generous green salad or the soup du jour, for example a hot and tasty broccoli soup, not overly thick, and lovely in color. French onion soup ($3.95), on the other hand, was disappointing, heavily seasoned with thyme and salt, and overwhelmed with a large thick crouton covered with cheese.

Our entrees were not very special either. The lamb ($21.95) was not very tender, and the fresh mahi mahi ($20.95) was flaky and moist but tasted bitter from the grill, with a sauce that seemed irrelevant to the flavor of the fish. Entrees come with a vegetable, as well as rice, pasta, or potato. The vegetables—celery, carrots, and cauliflower—were both crisp and attractive. Whole wheat rolls were warm and tasty.

Gaylord's wines are expensive, and the selection is limited to about a dozen French and about twice that number of California wines, with a Sutter Home White Zinfandel overpriced at $18. A Louis Latour Ardeche Chardonnay at $25 was a better buy than the three California chardonnays listed from $27.

Despite the drawbacks of the menu, however, the dining experience is still wonderful. Waiters in tuxedo shirts and cummerbunds are polite, attentive, and professional, and in the quiet courtyard, you escape the usual noisy distractions of clattering trays and banging dishes. Small details get lots of attention: water is served in elegant iced glasses with tangy lemon slices, and coffee cups are watched carefully. If you like to linger after dinner, you might want to bring a sweater, for temperatures can be chilly during winter months. And Gaylord's will dispatch its free limousine or van for special occasions.

Despite the pleasures of the evening, our bill for two with wine was close to $100 for a very ordinary meal which slid downhill after the first course. The best idea, as some friends advise, might be to order several appetizers and skip the entrees altogether!

With such an elegant setting, Gaylord's has the potential to develop into one of the island's truly special dining experiences, an image to haunt you when temperatures plunge back home. While we have found our dinners to be of uneven quality, however, we have heard high praise of Gaylord's lunch, where sandwiches, salads, and fresh seafood are reasonably priced ($6.95-$10) and you can look out at the garden in the full splendor of Hawaiian sunshine.

Lunch 11 am-4 pm. Dinner 5-10 pm daily. Light Supper 5-6:30 pm. with entrees from $12.95 with salad, rice, & vegetables. Children's full dinners ($9.95), usually beef, chicken, or fish. Children's full lunches ($3.75) including PBJ and grilled cheese. Sunday brunch 10 am-3 pm. Coffee: $1.00.

Kintaro

Walking into Kintaro is like entering a different world. The decor is serene and elegant, a tasteful harmony of blues, whites, grays and tans in perfect proportion. A fountain set in blue tiles and a sushi bar displaying a beautiful array of sashimi take up one long white wall. On nut-colored wood tables, set with chopsticks in blue and white wrappers, you'll find blue and tan tea bowls, and a striking single flower. Ceiling fans and air conditioning make Kintaro comfortably cool, and subdued Japanese music sets a relaxed mood. The total effect is bright, crisp, and immaculate.

What you choose to eat determines where you sit! If you want cocktails and pu pus, you can relax in a comfortable, attractive lounge, beautifully decorated in grays, light woods, and whites. You can sip a wonderful chi chi, sample elegant sashimi, or munch on crispy fried won tons from the owner's factory next door, and hot, tasty dumplings. You could almost make a meal of such treats!

In the same spacious room, you can try teppan yaki at specially designed tables and watch talented chefs chop and flip and make things sizzle right before your eyes. If you prefer the regular menu, you might be seated in the smaller, more intimate dining room.

No matter where you sit, your food will be delicious, attractive, and presented with impeccable attention to visual detail. Dinners include soup, rice, and sometimes a delicious seafood salad. Each meal is served with great politeness at a leisurely pace, from the first course of octopus and white cucumbers to the house dessert, green tea ice cream. Following a subtle and delicious miso soup, dinner entrees are presented on traditional sectioned wooden platforms and include rice, zaru soba (chilled buckwheat noodles with a special sauce) and pickled vegetables, along with tea served in a blue and tan pottery teapot. The intent is to present the diner with a sampling of varied tastes, with portions just the right size to tempt and satisfy rather than overwhelm the palate.

Kintaro is one of those rare restaurants that surprises you with each visit. The foods are so fresh and the preparation so subtle that you can confidently put your dinner in the hands of the owner and simply marvel at what he brings to the table. A sashimi platter arrived with six elegantly arranged selections, priced at $2.50 each: thin slices of ahi, translucent slivers of ono which were delicately sweet and fragrant, dark strips of pungent smoked salmon, shrimps cooked so perfectly that they seemed to melt as you tasted them, eel astonishingly sweet and tender. Garnished with pickled ginger, this was a sensational palette of tastes assembled with an eye for beauty as well as a taste for harmonies and contrasts.

During a recent visit, we tried the teppan yaki room, and watched the chef, in a dazzling display with twin shining steel spatulas, flip and scoot filets and vegetables across his sizzling grill. The ingredients, as you will see when they are presented to you in their raw form, are fresh and of the best quality. The teriyaki NY steak ($17.95) is tender, tasty and juicy. The lobster tail is excellent. The oysters lightly breaded and sauteed in olive oil ($13.95) are plump and tasty.

You won't be disappointed with the selections on the regular menu. Crispy shrimp tempura with vegetables ($12.95), for example, is delicious. Teriyaki beef made with slices of NY steak is exceptionally tender ($14). The beef sukiyaki in a cast iron pot ($13.75) was dark and dusky with translucent noodles, meat, and vegetables. Or try yose nabe ($11.50) , a Japanese bouillabaisse generous with seafood, vegetables, mushrooms, and yam noodles in a delicious broth. On one occasion, a fresh water trout, which friends had brought to the restaurant, was prepared with such finesse by the owner that every nose turned as he carried it to our table. While the green tea ice cream may please some but not others, a refreshing choice to complete the meal is Midori honey-dew melon liqueur, served either in a slender glass with a slice of lemon, or over ice cream. After dinner you can browse in the adjacent gift shop, which displays Japanese art, jewelry, and porcelains. Children are welcome, as is appropriate for a restaurant named in honor of a legendary Japanese boy hero, and everything seems arranged to be courteous, pleasant, and welcoming. For diners of any age, Kintaro is a must if you are looking for delicious Japanese food in an elegant, comfortable setting.

On Rt 56 in Wailua. House wine: Taylor California Cellars ($6.50). 5:30-9:30 pm daily. Reservations 822-3341. Credit Cards.

Kountry Kitchen

For years, the best spot for breakfast on the island's east coast has been the Kountry Kitchen, which serves terrific food at equally terrific prices. The large menu offers delicious eggs, expertly cooked bacon and sausage, as well as several omelette creations, including sour cream, bacon and tomato ($5.10) and vegetable garden ($5.30). You can even design your own omelette by ordering a combination of separately priced fillings. Kountry Kitchen's omelettes are unique—thin pancakes of egg rolled around fillings almost like a crepe—tender, moist, delicious. Our children usually choose Cheesy Eggs—toasted English muffin topped with bacon and poached eggs and covered with rich, golden cheese sauce ($4.20), and our babies have all loved the honey and wheat pancakes ($1.95), which are light and fragrant even when drowning in a small ocean of syrup. Hash browns are outstanding, perfectly golden and crisp pancakes of shredded potatoes, and portions are generous.

This very popular restaurant gets crowded at peak mealtimes; so plan to arrive a little early because tables get taken up very quickly, mostly by regular customers. The waitresses are pleasant and efficient and pour lots of absolutely delicious coffee. Across the street is a park with a sandy beach for walking afterwards.

The dinner menu features more than a dozen reasonably priced complete dinners, as well as five choices for children. Breakfast beverages include gourmet teas; at lunch or dinner you can order beer and wine. Go early to breakfast—the line is out the door by 8 am!

1485 Kuhio Hwy, just south of Kapa'a. 822-3511. Credit cards. Breakfast 6 am-9 pm daily. Coffee with cream $.75.

Kukui Nut Tree Inn

Air-conditioned, bright, and cheerful, the Kukui Nut Tree Inn looks more like California than Kauai. Bentwood chairs surround woodgrain tables, and lots of hanging and potted plants help to create a summer garden. The staff is as pleasant as the setting, and particularly helpful with small children. Our waitress complied readily with one child's request for a straw to go with her cup of cocoa and brought plenty of extra napkins at the same time. For breakfast, the ham and cheese omelette was generous and tasty, and the pancakes pleased our six-year old expert. The mushrooms in the omelette were fresh, and the coffee delicious.

Lunch is the busiest time because Kukui Nut Tree Inn attracts the business lunch crowd as well as exhausted shoppers. *Kapunas* (senior citizens) as well as *keikis* (children) have specially priced entrees which include soup or fruit cup; rice or potatoes; beverage, and dessert. The lunch menu is enormous, with 19 sandwiches, 23 lunch entrees (served either a la carte or for $2 more complete with soup) as well as salads and a generous bowl of saimin ($3.75). The kitchen's performance varies widely, and in the case of teriyaki beef, quality varies almost from slice to slice, with some tender and others intolerably fatty. Tempura ($5.95) was mushy, and the hot roast beef sandwich ($4.50) tough and tasteless. The bright spots were the french fries and the fried chicken, which was tender, hot, and crisp, as well as a generous and tasty club sandwich ($3.50). Don't miss the house special salad dressing made from papaya seeds, which has a delicious sweet and spicy taste similar to french. You can buy it to take home too. Although the food is not imaginative or distinctive, Kukui Nut Tree Inn is inexpensive and friendly. And after a hard morning of shopping, that may be all you need.

Kukui Grove Center, Lihue. Open daily for breakfast, lunch, and dinner except Sunday evenings. Credit cards. 245-7005.

Ma's Family Inc.

Ma's is a tiny luncheonette so far off the beaten path in Lihue that you'd probably never find it if you didn't stumble onto it by chance. For the past 18 years, the Japanese owners have established a reputation for well-priced and well-cooked breakfasts and lunches, and you'll probably find the dozen tables filled with local people on their way to work in the morning or stopping off for lunch. The few tourists who happen onto it will love Ma's expertly cooked eggs, delicious pancakes and waffles that our babysitter described as "about the best." The menu, which is posted on the wall over the pass-through to the kitchen, also lists some Hawaiian dishes, for example roast kalua pig that shredded perfectly for our little ones to pick up with their fingers. Even the toast is excellent. Corned beef hash lovers may find Ma's version too much like a potato pancake, but the fried min noodles accompanied by eggs and sausage may open your eyes to new possibilities for breakfast.

Service is fast and extremely friendly in the sunny, spartan dining room. Coffee arrives immediately in a large carafe and the food shortly thereafter. If you don't like canned milk in your coffee, ask for a small glass of the fresh stuff. When you leave, you'll be astonished to find how little your meal has cost you. When three adults and four children can breakfast for $14, you feel like popping into the kitchen to give Ma a big hug!

4277 Halenani St in Lihue (behind Kress Store on Rice St). Cash only. Open daily 5 am-1:30 pm. Weekends 12:30 am to 10 am. Coffee is free with breakfast!

Midori, Kauai Hilton

Midori, the gourmet restaurant in the Kauai Hilton, is full of surprises. Rather than the usual racks and tournedoes, you will find a highly personalized cuisine with a flair for the unexpected. Cream of taro leaf soup garnished with smoked ahi ($3.50), for example, or a complimentary pre-appetizer of sushi with flying fish eggs, pickled eggplant and strange and spicy cucumber. Unexpected tastes, to be sure, but differently delicious.

You will also find an unusually pretty restaurant, a private world of green and white, tucked away off the busy Hilton lobby and opposite a bustling sundry shop. Inside, Midori all is quiet elegance. Although you may still hear musicians playing too loudly in the lounge outside, they retire at 8:30 pm. Black lacquer chairs surround well-spaced tables adorned with white cloths and set with green and white china. Bonsai umbrella palms as well as Japanese fans and statues signal an oriental touch which is carried out subtly throughout the meal. Butter is served with chopsticks; Japanese mushrooms and fruits appear as garnishes.

Midori shows the careful control possible in a restaurant where few things are attempted in order to carry them out perfectly. The menu contains only thirteen entrees, from $15.50 (tempura vegetables) to $27.50 ("seafood experience"), and three are available as complete dinners with appetizer, soup or salad, entree, and dessert ($30). Though not extensive, the wine list is varied and well selected, with eleven California whites, most in the $20 range, and about thirty European whites, including a Chateau Moncontour Vouvray at $18, and a similar array of red wines from $12 to $37.

Whatever you select, be prepared for an adventure in taste and color. Small, braided herb-flavored rolls with goat cheese accompany the wonderful array of appetizers, like the lovely Midori salad ($5.50), with swirled shreds of carrot and cabbage arranged with goat cheese, avocado, tomato and oriental mushrooms, and accented with a dressing flavored with mint and lemon. A new item, Maui onion soup ($4) is wonderfully rich, dark and sweet, a generous bowl topped with cheese. Scampi ($7.75) is served on a bed of angel hair pasta, the four large shrimp very tender and perfectly matched with a delicately flavored sweet tomato sauce garnished with green onions. In Beef Samaurai ($6.75), a most elegant appetizer, thinly sliced beef is stir-fried with spicy vegetables and cellophane noodles and served inside a fresh cucumber. On our most recent visit, there were some disappointments (Midori's new chef was settling in): a miso soup, ($4) rather thin in flavor, and a duck breast salad ($6.75) more chewy than crisp.

After a sorbet of mango and lemon, the entrees are presented from a wheeled cart. The rack of lamb with pistachioes and zinfandel sauce ($20) is spectacular, the center of a colorful platter of pickled cabbage, snow peas, and shiitake mushrooms, and accompanied by sauteed whole baby squash, as well as potatoes which have been mashed, shaped and broiled. The effect is colorful, beautiful and tasty. The New York steak ($21.75) is equally wonderful, a large filet served with delicious sauce and so beautifully trimmed that what you could see you could eat entirely. Best of all, however, was the sauteed fresh ono ($17), so perfectly cooked that it was both crispy and moist, hot and fragrant. What made the dish special was a sauce of papaya, ginger, and lime so

magical that, rather than merely taking up space on the plate, it seemed somehow to release some secret, hidden splendor in the fish itself.

Desserts ($3.50) are also wonderful. The chocolate mousse layer cake is both light and chocolatey, but for an unusual choice, the tropical cheesecake with papaya and kiwi is unforgettable. Petit fours arrive with coffee, just one example of service which is extremely competent and friendly. Water comes in a glass with a slice of lemon and is replaced rather than refilled. The evening is so memorable that even a hefty bill ($85 for two with wine) seems worth it.

Among Kauai's gourmet restaurants, Midori has a distinct identity and cuisine. The oriental touch makes the menu special; prices are relatively reasonable; the dining room is quietly elegant. A good combination, and yet Midori is still more than the sum of its parts. It's unpretentious as well as understated, and that can make your dining experience somewhat more personal, and less like an opportunity for a professional staff to display its virtuosity.

In the Kauai Hilton Hotel. Credit cards. Jacket requested, not required. Coffee $1.75. Reservations 245-1955. Free valet parking. Closed Sundays.

Norberto's El Cafe

After many comfortable years in an old luncheonette tucked under the wing of the Roxy Theater, Norberto's has moved to more modern quarters on the main street of Kapa'a. The dining room is attractively laid out on two levels separated by beams and railings like a patio. White stucco walls and woodgrain tables create a setting like a cantina, colorfully decorated with hanging plants, sombreros, and gas lamps. Trophies won by the girls' softball team, coached by Norberto, sit atop a piano, where guests occasionally contribute to the informal atmosphere with impromptu entertainment.

Over the years, prices have not changed much, and almost everything is very reasonable. Bud on tap, served in a full pitcher with iced beer mugs, is only $4.50. Margaritas go for $1.50 (or $2.50 in a beer mug and $8.50 for a pitcher!), and even the Taylor California Cellars at $5/carafe is bargain priced. For dinner, El

Cafe offers a variety of inexpensive a la carte choices as well as 6 complete Mexican dinners with soup, vegetable, beans, chips and salsa for $9.95 or less. Sensational guacamole is only $1.50, or half price with a dinner! The terrific nachos ($2.00/small) are generously covered with cheese and perfectly flavored with chilis. When we finished our bean soup ($1.75), we were even asked if we wanted seconds!

The Burrito El Cafe ($6.95) truly deserves to be called a house specialty—the tortilla generously stuffed with flavorful beef, beans and cheese, baked enchilada style and topped with guacamole and the freshest red tomatoes and lettuce. On the full dinner menu, the tostada ($8.95) was a huge colorful salad mounded over a crisp tortilla, and Norberto's famous Chili Relleno ($8.95) steals the show —a chili dipped (not drowned) in egg and gently cooked, so that it comes to you as light and tender as a crepe, and so delicately flavored that you'll wonder just what magic show Norberto has going on back there in his kitchen! For a perfect finale, try some delicious homemade rum cake ($1.50). Norberto's meat dishes can also be ordered vegetarian style. For the some who like it hot, plenty of homemade salsa is on the table to add to your dishes, and the chef will be happy to say "Ole!" to any challenge!

Service is friendly, and children are treated with tolerance. When Mikey announced his order for chicken without anything like a tortilla to wreck the taste, he was served a small bowl of chicken suitably pure. El Cafe is the best Mexican restaurant on the island, and well worth the spectacular drive to Kapa'a if you are staying in Poipu or Hanalei.

4-1373 Kuhio Hwy, (cross street: Kukui St) in the heart of historic Kapa'a town. 822-3362. 5:30-9:30 pm daily. Children's complete dinners $4.50. Coffee $.75.

Olympic Cafe

For years, the Olympic Cafe has looked too modern for weatherbeaten old Kapa'a. Clean paint and windows shaped like Japanese lanterns right next door to ramshackle roofs and rusted Coca Cola signs? But the Olympic was just ahead of its time, and proves once more that, if you are patient, the world will catch up with you. Kapa'a has been discovered as "quaint," and as the town enters the tourist era with a spurt of building and renovation, it's just catching up with the Olympic and a hard working Japanese family with foresight!

Inside, the tan and white room is comfortably cool with fly fans, the woodgrain formica tables roomy and clean. Prices are reasonable. For $1.95, you can have the breakfast special—2 pancakes, an egg, and 2 strips of bacon, just enough to make short people cheerful. The corned beef hash is a bit heavy on the potatoes, but still tasty. Coffee is excellent, though you have to settle for Royal Danish creamer or order a side of milk! For a quick meal on a morning when you want to play with the sand rather than your silverware, the Olympic may be your best bet!

Rt 56, in Kapa'a. Breakfast and lunch 7 am-2 pm daily. Dinner 5-9 pm. Coffee $.50. Lunch and dinner daily.

Ono Family Restaurant

The Ono Family Restaurant specializes in wholesome, inexpensive family fare. Breakfasts are well cooked, attractively served, and generous, including some house specialties which are really special. Eggs Vegie ($4.75) is a version of eggs benedict with fresh sauteed zucchini instead of meat. The pancakes ($2.55/ adult; $1.50/ child)) were voted "Ex!" by our six-year-old expert, and we all had a chance to help her finish her portion. The ham and cheese omelette ($5.35) was soft and delicious. Our waitress was very helpful with things like crackers, straws, extra napkins and extra cups for tastes of grown-up coffee—those etceteras of family dining that don't seem essential until they're missing.

For lunch, children's plates are a bargain and include a a cup of soup and a beverage. A children's chicken platter ($3.50), for example, includes a leg and thigh baked in a sweet barbecue sauce. Adults will find the hamburgers, priced from $3.65 ($2.50/ child), on the whole competently cooked, and anyone on a diet will be pleased with the vegie combo sandwich ($4.55) served on wheat branola bread. The buffalo burgers (from $5.25) are more lean and healthy than beef for the cholesterol conscious, and their distinctive flavor will please some but not others (and unfortunately not our children)! You might also try the delicious Portuguese bean soup ($1.55), spicy with sausage, beans and macaroni. French fries are hot and crispy, and the lemonade is the real thing!

The restaurant has a cozy, friendly atmosphere. Wooden booths shine with polish, and many feature a partition which can be removed in order to connect two together and seat a large family like ours. Gold carpeting, pleasant yellow walls with paneling, cheerful curtains, and flowers make the dining room attractive. The family's antiques harmonize with a homey assortment of square and round tables. Air conditioning keeps temperatures comfortable, or you can sit outside on a patio enclosed by wrought iron grillwork.

Although at times service can be painfully slow, everyone is friendly and cooperative. While you wait, children can work on pencil puzzles provided on their menus, and people seem ready to help with each other's restless little ones. On one occasion, when we could not find our waitress to get a glass of water that had suddenly become an urgent necessity, an adjacent Daddy passed over an extra. Just outside the open door, two old timers shared their donuts with our wandering five-year-old, patted her head as she chewed, and listened politely to her latest fish story.

4-1292 Kuhio Hwy, Kapa'a. Open 7 am - 9 pm except Mondays. Closed Sundays at 2 pm. Credit cards. 822-1710. Coffee $.75.

The Planters

Just a few feet off Rt 56 at Hanama'ulu, The Planters is in an improbable spot for a restaurant featuring patio dining. The patio is the non-smoking dining area, which is probably cooler than the interior in summer, but its location next to the parking lot gives diners an excellent view of the cars. Inside this historic plantation building is a dining room ventilated by ceiling fans and decorated with sugar plantation memorabilia—machinery parts and tools, horse collars and ox yokes, and even a red wagon wheel hung with lanterns and plants. Candles shine on wood plank tables, and at the rear, two private booths with black leatherette couches cozy up to an indoor waterfall.

More than a dozen dinners, including three New Orleans style "blackened" dishes, range from $8.95 for chicken teriyaki up to

$24.95 for steak and lobster. Entrees come with soup or salad, as well as rice, potato, or a somewhat garlicky pasta with romano cheese. Children can choose prime rib, chicken or shrimp dinners for only $5.95, and the boneless chicken breast passed the most stringent "no-gook" test from the small picky eaters. For the first course, you get a bowl, which can be filled with either salad or a seafood chowder. Though chunky with fish and vegetables, the soup was rather bland without a few turns of the pepper mill to liven it up. The dinner salad included carrots, cucumbers and tomatoes. You also get french bread, toasted with or without garlic, but the absence of bread plates means that in short order you'll have crumbs skittering everywhere. We found house specialty prime rib to be tasty and tender, served with good au jus but no bone, and certainly reasonably priced at $12.95. The steamed lobster tail, on the other hand, was tender though not distinctive enough to merit the $19.95 price. Macadamia nut pie ($2.50) was overly sweet. The wine list has only eight selections, with the top-priced wine, a Beringer Chardonnay,$15.

Planters is obviously not the place to order an expensive meal. Your plan should be to spend as little possible and to stick to the basics, like the chicken and prime rib. In fact, some local people recommend the prime rib sandwich, a bargain at only $7.95, and available at both lunch and dinner.

On Rt 56 in Downtown Hanama'ulu. 245-1606. Open 11 am-3:30 pm and 5-9:45 pm daily (open for dinner only on Sundays).

Prince Bill's, Westin Kauai

At Prince Bill's, you will be dining at the only penthouse restaurant on Kauai. On the top floor of the Westin's tower, the dining room has a sweeping view of Kalapaki Bay, and from a window table, you can watch the waves roll in slender lines of foam and break far below you. The room is lovely, although you will find it hard to take your eyes off the view, especially in moonlight, when clouds rimmed with silver steal silently across the sky to hide the moon. In another moment, the moon escapes to light the glistening sea and cast lovely moonshadows on the gardens below. Prince Bill's enjoys this spectacular perch because the tower, part of the old Kauai Surf Hotel, was built before strict zoning regulations limited construction to four stories—"no higher than a coconut tree."

Prince Bill's is an improvement over the former occupant of this enviable spot, the Kauai Surf's Golden Cape Restaurant. The new peach and white decor emphasizes the spaciousness of the tall ceilings and of the two-level design of the dining room which allows almost everyone a gorgeous view. Even better, the giant windows can now be opened, and you can enjoy wonderful breezes as well as the the sounds of the surf.

Prince Bill's is especially lovely at breakfast. As you look down on palm trees and golden sand and feel the gentle morning breezes, you'll be thinking of all you want to do at the beach, although it's hard to leave a breakfast buffet with so many delicious creations. You'll find strawberry blintzes and baked apples, smoked sturgeon with capers, Banger and link sausages, wonderful fresh fruits and juices, pastries and fruit breads, or an omelette created before your eyes with your favorite cheeses and vegetables. Breakfast is not only delicious but elegantly served on white linen tablecloths set with fresh flowers. Champagne arrives in lovely glasses, and the staff is exceptionally friendly and helpful, especially to children who need assistance carrying plates. Our ten-year-old could not believe his eyes when the catsup he requested was ceremoniously carried to the table balanced on a tiny saucer! These little people on their best behavior were also delighted when Gerald, our cordial waiter, served hot chocolate to each one in a miniature silver pot. Afterwards, while parents enjoy the champagne and and count the waves rolling into the bay, youngsters can go downstairs to explore the pool, and this excursion is an adventure in itself, as they have to follow complex directions based on the color of the columns! For all this entertainment, the buffet price ($16 for adults; $9.50 for children) seems well worth it, and if you have a plate of fruit and pastry plus beverage, the cost is only $7.25.

At dinner, Prince Bill's looks like a different restaurant, open at twilight to evening breezes which make the candle flames dance romantically in their glass holders. The windows open to the starry sky, with moonlight floating like a silver net across the sea. In the quiet dining room, you can hear the sound of the waves breaking far below you in gentle rhythms.

The menu features a dozen four-course dinners which cost between $25 and $35. Entree choices include certified Black Angus steaks and prime rib, fresh fish, chicken, lamb, and lobster. Dinner begins with a visit to the appetizer buffet where you'll find colorful vegetable and seafood salads, ahi sashimi and calamari, cold cuts, and a mountain of cooked shrimps served in the shell with cocktail sauce. Eating them is sticky business, which makes you grateful for the hot towels that follow! Caesar salad is next, creditably done despite the need for bulk preparation, and fresh-baked country french bread and sweet butter. Also in the basket is delicious coconut bread served with fragrant orange honey butter. It's so much like pound cake that you could save it for dessert, or if you prefer, you can visit the dessert bar ($4.50) where too many delicious looking pastries are full of too many calories for comfort! We tried a sensational cream tart topped with four perfectly ripe, perfectly round balls of papaya. After dinner, you can linger over delicious coffee, listen to Hawaiian melodies, and gaze out at sea.

The kitchen does very well with the menu. Two generous 3-bone lamb chops ($30) were perfectly crisp yet moist, very tender and tasty. Though the sauteed fresh ono ($29) was on the dry side, the prime rib ($28) was tender and juicy, cooked to order and delicious. The New York steak ($28), certified Black Angus beef, was also first rate. With the entrees come ripe tomatoes provencale, a crock of thin, very flaky au gratin potatoes attractively served in a copper pan, and fresh vegetables, in our case ginger carrots and sugar peas with straw mushrooms and onions. Service is skilled as well as friendly. Your meal is never hurried, and every effort is made to make each aspect of your dining experience as pleasant as possible.

The wine list features most of the wines in the Westin's other restaurants, yet at prices oddly enough about a half-dollar or so less. Many of the California 1986 and 1987 vintages cost under $18, and if you feel like spending more, Sonoma Cutrer Russian River Chardonnay is $30.

Prince Bill's offers a unique and spectacular setting, delicious food, and polite, professional service. Though the menu is not inexpensive, you get a good value for your money. You won't go away hungry, and you will most likely remember an evening of good food laced with romantic images—the sounds of the sea, the foam on the waves, and the touch of tropical evening breezes.

In the Westin Kauai Hotel. Reservations necessary. Informal attire. Breakfast Buffet $16/adults; $9.50/children. Continental breakfast $7.25.

Rosita's

There's enough on Rosita's menu for the whole family. It offers the largest menu of any Mexican restaurant on Kauai, and in addition to the usual tortillas and tacos, diners can choose lasagne, hamburgers, steaks, fresh fish, chicken and pork at prices less than $10. Children can have a creditable hamburger and fries ($3.50), hot dog ($2.95)or chicken, taco, or enchilada.

Rosita's also has a pleasant dining room in the Kukui Grove Shopping Center in Lihue. White stucco walls, green leafy plants, and dark stained wood tables with tiles create a comfortable, informal setting. Stained glass lanterns provide soft light, and iron grillwork along with murals of vaguely southwestern landscape set an ethnic tone. In front, the bar is a pleasant, attractive spot to enjoy outstanding margaritas or delicious sangria, available in a full liter with no ice and lots of limes ($8). Semi-enclosed booths with straight-backed benches line the walls, and because the wood benches are connected, they can be a problem when the restaurant is crowded. If someone at one table moves down, whoever is sitting at the adjacent table moves up!

Over the years we've had mixed experiences at Rosita's. Sometimes the food was so hot you could feel the steam in your ears; at other times, spicing was just how we ordered it. Sometimes the service has been quick and good-humored, but at other times the reverse. Food quality has been equally variable. The Deluxe Burrito ($6.50) has varied from delicious to pasty, and the Chimichanga ($5.95) has been sometimes dry and tasteless, but on our most recent visit crisp and stuffed with tasty filling. Some years we have criticized the kitchen for being stingy with the guacamole ($4.25), because what looked like a full cup was actually mounded on top of at least an inch of shredded lettuce, but

on our last visit we found the portion generous as well as delicious. One dish has never varied: the nachos ($4) have been unfailingly delicious, an enormous portion of cheesy chips perfectly flavored with chilis. The teriyaki chicken dinner ($8.50) was tasty, though unaccountably stingy on the meat.

Over the past several years, both both food quality and service at Rosita's have been at best uneven. For this reason, adults might seek other places to spend a quiet evening together. On the other hand, families with children are almost sure to find Rosita's a friendly place to enjoy generous portions of adequate food, and for the benefit of picky short eaters, the widest menu selection of any Mexican restaurant on Kauai.

Kukui Grove Shopping Center, Lihue. Reservations 245-8561. Credit cards. Coffee $.65. Open 11:30 am–3 pm and 5:30–10 pm.

The Seashell

There's good news at the Seashell: a new, more reasonably priced menu! After a two-year experiment, management has decided to discontinue the separate charge for the salad bar, a policy that jacked up the price of each dinner by $3, and made the Seashell more expensive than most other island seafood restaurants. Entrees are reasonably priced and selected. Chicken breast has come down a dollar in price to $14.95, and for the first time, a menu has been added for the ten-and-under set, featuring chicken nuggets, "spaghettietti" and hamburger with fries for $6 or less. Unfortunately, the only bargain on the old menu, the popular "popcorn shrimp" once available in an all-you-can-eat portion, has disappeared. A new wine list offers 25 wines, most from California and most priced under $20. You could hardly call this menu inexpensive, however. Fresh fish is still $17.50 and the least expensive entree is a seafood pasta dish for $12.95.

We started with sashimi, a generous portion of thinly sliced ahi which was meltingly tender. Deep fried calamari ($3.95) served in a large white shell was crisp and tasty. Deep fried zucchini ($3.75) was hot and moist, although retaining a bit too much oil for first-rate "tempura-style" as described in the menu. As a better complement to its delicate flavor, you might request the sauce for sashimi instead of the strong cocktail sauce which comes with it.

A better choice on the complete dinner than the rather bland seafood chowder, the salad bar is extensive, and everything is attractively displayed—huge bowls of fresh spinach and lettuce, large clam shells filled very red tomatoes, fresh vegetables, giant mushrooms vinaigrette, pasta and vegetable salads.

The kitchen specializes in fresh fish, and we have learned in the past to avoid any dishes which require sauces or subtlety, for seasoning is often heavy handed. This was true with the ono, which was much better without the strong wine and butter sauce that came with it. Surprisingly, however, we found the fish somewhat bitter from the grill, so you might consider ordering your filet sauteed, and only in plain butter. The sauteed fresh ahi, for example, had much better taste, though it was not as flavorful as we have found on previous visits. We enjoyed the scallops sauteed with mushrooms, vegetables and ginger ($16.25), for the scallops were tasty and not overcooked, and the sauce enhanced rather than disguised their flavor. Cioppino ($15.75) was another excellent choice, the fish, clams, shrimps and scallops cooked only to tenderness, and the broth piquant and light, colorful with snow peas, celery, carrots and onions. The New York steak arrived perfectly cooked, tender and juicy, though looking a bit small (8 oz for $16.50). We were disappointed, however, with the lobster tail, priced at a whopping $25.50, and served so undercooked that it had to be sent back twice. So large and thick a tail is difficult to broil without drying it out, which the chef was clearly trying to avoid, but either a different size (two smaller tails, for example) or a different process (like steaming) might lead to greater success.

Despite its modest, unpretentious exterior, The Seashell is not an inexpensive restaurant when you add in appetizers, cocktails, coffee and dessert. If your mood is informal, it may be just the right place, for the food is fine, the dining room pleasantly decorated, and the service friendly from waitpersons dressed in snazzy turquoise shirts and white trousers. If you're looking for something special, however, and willing to drive to find it, consider spending a few dollars more at Inn on the Cliffs at the Westin, at The House of Seafood or Brennecke's Beach Broiler in Poipu, or at Hanalei Dolphin on the north shore.

On Rt 56 in Wailua, opposite Coco Palms Hotel. Reservations essential (request a window table but be prepared to wait for it): 822-3632. Dinner 5:30–10 pm daily. Coffee/brewed decaf $1.50.

Restaurant Shiroma

In a tiny shopping center on Rt 56 near Kapa'a, Restaurant Shiroma has been popular with local families for years. Three meals a day are cooked in a tiny kitchen and served at small tables to people with large appetites and tight budgets. Although not every dish is equally tasty (in fact, some dishes cooked by the friendly Oriental owners are on the salty side), the saimin is among the best on the eastern shore, the noodles tender and tasty and the broth rich and flavorful. Wun tun min ($2.85) comes with four delicious wun tuns and slender slices of tasty pork. Steak teriyaki is another favorite, large slices of soft and tender beef with an excellent teriyaki flavor. Fried wun tuns are crispy and full of delicious soft filling. If you don't want to eat at one of the half-dozen formica tables in the warm dining room, phone your order in ahead and take it to the beach for lunch on the sand!

971-C Kuhio Hwy, Wailua. 822-0111.

The Sizzler

From the road, the Sizzler's red roof and green and white awnings are a cheerful invitation to come inside. Beneath those awnings, however, we found a sizzling disappointment! First, you must stand on line while an employee takes down the orders of everyone ahead of you. Then you pay—in cash—while your order is called into the kitchen at the register. With receipt in hand, you find a table, then visit the famous salad bar which costs extra unless you are a senior citizen. That much is predictable. The rest is up to chance. Your food may be brought out too soon or, if the restaurant is full, later than you'd like, and as we found on two occasions, without everything you ordered, so don't lose that proof of purchase in the salad dressing! And prices are deceptive. What looks like a great buy on the sign outside (Prime Rib Dinner $8.99) is, according to our waiter, only 8 oz—not much to look at on the plate, and it's more than $10 if you add the salad bar. If you add the salad bar to the larger prime rib ($15.99), you'll actually pay a whopping $18.28— more than you would at the Bull Shed ($16.95), which offers a salad bar and also table service. The best bargains seem to be the "all you can eat" barbecue ribs (11.59) or shrimp ($10.99) which come with a small steak, and you won't have to wait long for refills, because waiters circulate with baskets of shrimps and ribs looking for appropriate empty plates!

Although our children loved the hot chocolate ($.93) and the teriyaki "hibachi chicken" ($6.79), which was very tender, tasty, and moist, other entrees left them cold. The New York steak seemed small for 10 oz and was not very tasty ($8.89). At $6.79, the salad bar with soup is probably the best deal.

At breakfast, you'll find the same line, the same system, and the same problems. Food orders don't always arrive at the same time, and service is uneven. When our older children went to Sizzler on a great adventure—breakfast without Mom and Dad—even they had mixed experiences. One morning, the waiter offered them fruit from the salad bar when their breakfasts were delayed more than twenty minutes. Another morning, however, the waitress brought the wrong order for one child, and cold eggs for the others. She whisked the eggs back to the kitchen, but the eggs came back reheated rather than recooked. At that point, the children told her, with all the grave politeness of short people trying to act tall, that the eggs were as hard as rocks and the papaya slices were hot. The waitress, however, informed them that the eggs could not be returned more than once!

At the Sizzler, you have to work for what you eat, and dining is rushed rather than relaxed. As in many fast food outlets, you'll find the dining room clean and bright, but it's hard to imagine wanting to linger over coffee for very long. You end up, in our opinion, paying too much for too little, and all of it in precious vacation cash. For these reasons, we found the Sizzler, alas, to be a fizzler!

On Rt 56 in Wailua. No reservations or credit cards. Cocktails, wine, and beer. Breakfast, lunch, and dinner daily.

Tempura Garden, Westin Kauai

At Tempura Garden, the Westin has bypassed the tradition of Benihana in favor of the tradition of *kaiseki,* the exquisitely fine dining developed over centuries by Kyoto's noble class. Ceremony and presentation are as important as what is eaten, and each element of the meal is carefully chosen as part of the total composition of color, texture and taste. Ingredients are the finest and freshest of the season; natural flavors and colors are enhanced rather than disguised by seasonings; and every aspect of the meal is designed to achieve an elegant simplicity which belies the extraordinary effort involved in the preparation.

On the menu you will find three *kaiseki* dinners ($25-$39), each a different level of entry into this exotic cuisine. Each includes perhaps nine courses: appetizer, sliced raw fish, clear soup, tempura, broiled selection, vinegared salad, steamed rice, pickled vegetables, final soup, fresh fruit desert, ceremonial green tea, and confectionery. Our host, David, suggested "Kamogawa" ($33/person) as containing foods most accessible to Western palates, and we decided to put ourselves confidently in his hands and plunge ahead into the unknown.

From start to finish of this extraordinary dining experience, the colors and shapes delight the eye while tastes and textures intrigue the palate. Our first course, a fish cake topped with sea urchin roe, was delicate and light. Next came sliced raw fish, both ahi (yellow fin tuna) and a deliciously subtle white fish (yellow tail), the translucent slices arranged on single leaf of shiso, an herb with a wonderful fragrance of mint and anise. Our third course was a clear soup with a single, floating fish cake. Our broiled entree, pink snapper, was perfectly cooked, very sweet, and garnished with pungent shredded shiitake mushrooms. Tempura followed, impossibly light, almost confections of shrimp and white fish, eggplant and mushrooms. The vinegar salad of clam, shrimp and persimmon was a piquant counterpoint, and then the 'final soup,' richly flavored miso soup served warm rather than hot, and white rice in a lacquer bowl.

Not everyone has to order a full *kaiseki* dinner. You can sample some of the same foods if you choose the Tempura Dinner, a seven-course meal priced according to the tempura entree selection ($24-$37), or the Bento dinner ($28), a six-course meal of tempura, sashimi, and broiled entree served partly in an elegant lacquer box with three drawers, each opening, like a surprise, to reveal a beautiful display. In one drawer, for example, shredded chicken is artfully arranged with Japanese radish and red caviar; or in another drawer, you may find tender poached chicken, skewered shrimp and a single quail egg. You can also choose from a la carte tempura selections ($2.50-$5), or broiled, steamed, or simmered dishes priced around $8.

The dining room has the understated elegance suitable as a backdrop for the spectacular colors and artistic presentation of the cuisine. Plain wood floors and black marble counters and tables seem at once luxurious and spare. Everything is also authentic, from the elegant Japanese china to the lacquer platters painted with a single white orchid to mark each diner's place. Except for a half dozen tables in the rear, most of the dining takes place at a long counter, where people who sit side by side can watch the chefs slice and chop and make things sizzle. A unique feature of this restaurant, the cooking staff includes graduates of the culinary school of Kyoto, who come to the Westin to complete their training under the supervision of Chef Kunio Nakamura of the Academy of Taiwan Gaku-en, who brings in special supplies twice weekly from Japan.

Dining at Tempura Garden is clearly not for everyone. The cuisine is highly specialized as well as expensive. Large parties will find it difficult to converse if they are seated side by side at the counter, and should reserve one of the few tables well in advance. The restaurant is somewhat more noisy than the tranquil garden setting you'd expect from its name and tradition. The sound of water splashing in the garden outside can be distracting, and the system of cooking ventilation inside adds additional volume. Surprisingly, it's the only indoor Westin restaurant that is not air-conditioned, although fly fans can usually keep the air moving.

At Tempura Garden, the cuisine is superb and the service elegant—and you can enjoy a meal you'd find nowhere else on Kauai.

Reservations 245-5050. Free valet parking. Credit cards.

The Masters, Westin Kauai

You may think it's only another three-figure meal, but at the Masters, it will be a complete evening's experience that you are paying for, and it begins at the hotel lobby entrance when the valet takes your car, your keys, and your other life, and parks them. From then on, your welfare is in the hands of staff. You are carried to the restaurant in a limousine, or even a horse-drawn carriage, by a chauffeur who politely asks your opinion of the weather. Or, if you prefer, you can cruise the hotel's lagoon in a mahogany launch handcrafted in Venice! Whatever vehicle you choose, the door will be opened by a uniformed, ribbon-sashed escort who will most likely inquire about your day as he walks you to the restaurant door, where he will solemnly hand you over to the maitre de or captain who will assume the responsibility for negotiating your safe arrival at your table. Waiters appear soundlessly to move your chair and open your napkin. It has been a seamless web of service, and it will all occur again, in reverse, when you leave.

This is all great fun, an aperitif of sparkling self-importance, and the main course is a spectacular cuisine created by chef Pierre Lecoutre, brought over from France to open the restaurant at Christmas, 1987. Although he stayed for less than a year, he completed the work of designing the menu, which changes with each season, and training a staff.

The menu offers about a dozen a la carte entrees in classical preparations, as well as two prix fixe dinners: a three-course dinner for $60 per person and a five-course dinner for $15 more. If you choose the a la carte menu, you will discover that two of the nine appetizers contain duck liver, one of those foods about which few people are neutral. At the suggestion of the maitre de, we shared the chef's specialty, Truffle Surprise ($20), a ball of duck liver rolled in truffles and finished with an aspic of duck, and the surprise was ours, for this dish was the smoothest, creamiest, most delicious creation imaginable, and more special than the sauteed

foie gras with cognac sauce ($19). The lobster salad ($16) was almost as wonderful, the lobster still warm and meltingly tender, served with endives and fresh local manoa lettuce and garnished with julienned mushrooms in a lobster tarragon vinaigrette.

As the menu changes with each season, the preparation of the same basic fish and meat selections varies. For example, on *Le Menu d'Hiver,* the rack of lamb ($37) may be roasted with mustard and rosemary, while on *Le Menu de l'Automne,* the lamb may appear in three elegant chops decked with a medley of wood mushrooms—chanterelles, truffles, and shiitake—each marvelously flavorful, in a dark, rich sauce which perfectly complemented the lamb. You will also find at least two fresh island fish on the menu. In one version, the fresh mahi mahi is served with a deliciously subtle champagne sauce and garnished with a beautiful medallion of lobster and a fish mousse. You may find papio ($31), flawlessly poached and served with three distictly flavored and colorful sauces. We have been disappointed in only one fish preparation, a poached opakapaka ($26) served with a cabernet sauvignon sauce, in our opinion too strong in flavor and color for such a delicate fish.

But it is the spectacle of the meal, the truffles and flourishes, which will leave the dominant impression. Your water goblet will be filled with bottled evian, your silver changed with each course, and each delicacy served from large silver trays in dishes with domed silver lids. There will be fresh fruit sorbet to cleanse the palate and on your bread plate a succession of single, perfectly crisp slices of bread served with great ceremony from a basket cunningly crafted of a country loaf. A server seems never more than an elbow away, yet so unobtrusive as to seem to vanish into thin air, to elusive melodies played gently by an accomplished harpist.

The dining room is an elegant setting for all this luxury. In scale it seems larger than life. Tall carved ceilings are intricately contoured like canopies over four banks of tables, each divided by etched glass into four dining compartments. To soften the grand lines of this chamber, there are curves everywhere, curves in the shape of the tall paned windows, curves in in the columns and arches. Each table is large, covered with a lace cloth, lit with candles and adorned with fresh roses and tuberoses. White napkins are clasped with silver rings. It looks the price, as does the wine list, where you can find some selections costing several hundred dollars and one, clearly the most valuable bottle on Kauai, for more than a thousand! Most of the reasonably priced wines are 1986 and 1987 vintages, with several good choices for under $20.

Those who remember The Masters' master chef will miss him not so much in the bold strokes, but in the smallest shadings of the cuisine. While vegetables remain expertly prepared, for example, one misses the wit and sparkle which could envision and devise such wonders as a small ratatouille wrapped in spinach or a flan of fresh vegetables sweet with carrots and tangy with chives. Or, for dessert, two balls of plain and a third of coffee-flavored meringue, served with a fragrant coffee custard sauce.

The Masters is as expensive as any first-rate mainland restaurant, and this is very expensive for Kauai. On the most recent menu, entrees ranged from $31 to $42, and appetizers from $7 to $19. The changing menu has been an opportunity for changing prices, which have gone up in some cases, as in Truffle Surprise, as much as 25% over the last year. It's still possible for two to get away with less than the three figures, but you'll have to order with restraint. For example, a fine and subtle consomme with sherry costs only $7 for a cup, or two can share a single Truffle Surprise. By reducing the cost of the appetizer, ordering two glasses of wine instead of a bottle, and skipping coffee and dessert, two can have a memorable dinner for about $50 per person. Only you can decide whether spending that figure—and probably more—is going to make you smile or scowl when your credit card bill arrives in the mail!

In the Westin Kauai. 245-5050. Free valet parking. Credit cards.

Tip Top Motel

With a name like Tip Top, this combination motel, restaurant, and bakery conjures up certain expectations: a clean room for under $20, a square meal for under $5. But you're not really sure that such a belief is any more justified than faith in the tooth fairy. It is true, though. Since 1916, the Tip Top Motel has served fairly priced, honest and unpretentious food, and for this reason, is more popular with local people than the tourists who manage to find it on the side street of Lihue. The dining room is large and dimly lit, with the dull, hollow sound of a school cafeteria, but nonetheless it is comfortably air-conditioned, with booths along the wall and well spaced formica tables. The real attraction is the prices. Delicious pancakes with macadamia nuts, bananas, pineapples or raisins are only $2.25. Bacon and eggs, accompanied by a scoop of hash browns, cost $2.95. A ham and cheese omelette is $3.35. While in general the food is well-prepared if unexciting, the homemade pineapple and guava jam is special. Have it on toast, but that's a la carte.

Children will have fun here. They can roam around, check out the bakery display or select postcards from the rack while breakfast is being prepared. Our waitress, a grandmother who had raised twelve children of her own, was unusually tolerant, patient and kind, making an extra trip to the bakery to switch donuts when our six–year–old changed her mind and was on the verge of tears. The donuts are delicious—take some along for a snack—and be sure to sample the house specialty, macadamia nut cookies. At Tip Top, you won't find the kind of breakfasts you get at Kountry Kitchen or Eggbert's, but you won't pay their prices either. And what you do get is good enough to keep everyone cheerful—until lunch!

3173 Akahi St, Lihue. Cash. Coffee $.60. Opens daily at 6:45 am.

Tropical Taco

For years, the green truck parked in Hanalei was famous for serving the finest fish tacos west of Mexico, and when Tropical Taco opened a restaurant and cantina, the emphasis was on cantina. An enormous bar was the predominant decorative feature, and light rock set the mood for margaritas and chips. Now, the addition of a second small dining room located farther from the bar makes dining quieter and more comfortable for families.

Although the pink stucco walls and green floors and rafters may remind no one of Mexico, the decor fits the 'tropical' version, just right for sunsets and palm trees. It's a warm spot, however, despite the fly fans, for you're in a shopping center where breezes seem as frequent as elephants. But here you'll find the best fish taco anywhere, the fresh ono absolutely sensational with a hint of cilantro, and the price an unbeatable $3.25. Or you can walk into the back and take your taco out, just as you had to do in the old days, at the very spot where many a tortilla crossed to a hungry hombre!

In the Kapa'a Shopping Center next to Big Save. 11 am - 9:30 pm. Closed Sundays. Credit cards. Take out: 822-3622.

The Voyage Room, Sheraton Coconut Beach Hotel

The centerpiece of the Voyage Room's menu is a dinner buffet ($15.55) which includes carved roast beef as well as four additional hot entrees, dessert, beverage, and the extensive salad bar which has always been the Voyage Room's best feature. The rest of the menu is still very expensive, with the "Bill of Fare" for a complete dinner a rousing $27, for which you get a bowl of soup or "tossed green salad" (not a visit to the salad bar), shrimp cocktail, dessert, and beverage. Less expensive a la carte choices start at $12.95 for mahi mahi (frozen, not fresh). The daily specials ($9.95) are a relative bargain. During our last visit, we had a choice of spaghetti or fresh fish.

Food quality is average, and if you're looking for plain cooking, you won't find it here. Chicken and shrimp are either deep fried, for example, or baked and stuffed. The roast beef can best be described as inoffensive, while the barbecued chicken was bland. The fresh ono ($9.95 on the special) though generous and reasonably tender was nothing remarkable, and you should have all sauce and capers left on the side (or better, in the kitchen!). An unexpected treat: the best fresh onion rolls we have found!

One of the best values on the island is still the Voyage Room salad bar by itself, a spectacular array of fruits, cheeses, and fresh vegetables for only $7.50. Or combine it with a crock of hot, tasty onion soup thick with cheese ($3.25). The wine list, though unbelievably limited, offers a 1985 Chateau St. Michelle Fume Blanc for only $13.95.

The ups and downs of this changeable restaurant have certainly kept us busy. We always look forward to our return visits, not only because we never know just what we'll find, but also because the Voyage Room is such a pleasant place for dinner and conversation. Even when full, the dining room feels uncrowded, the tall and roomy rattan chairs screening other diners from view, and the tiered arrangement of tables creating privacy. Gentle breezes from the hotel's central courtyard keep the temperature cool, and candle flames glow romantically on tables set with white linen and shining glassware. This is a place to go when the moon is full, for you can sit on the veranda and watch the leaves dance in a luminous sky to the music of a fountain. After dinner, stroll along the beach and count the silver linings of the clouds, or watch as silver spreads across the waves when the moon steals free to light the sky.

In the Sheraton Coconut Beach, Kapa'a. Reservations 822-4422. Credit Cards. Coffee $1.25. House wine: Inglenook $8.50/$4.50. Children's dinners on selected entrees.

Wailua Marina Restaurant

One of the oldest restaurants on Kauai, the Wailua Marina is also one of the best inexpensive places to take the family. Though owned by relatives of the family which operates the Green Garden Restaurant in Hanapepe (you'll recognize the placemats!), the Marina has a completely separate identity and, in our opinion, much better food. The dining room is large and features an enormous mural of an underwater vista complete with stuffed fish and a turtle shell. Weather permitting, ask to sit on the large covered porch decorated with plants and fresh flowers. Cooled by delightful breezes, it looks out over the Wailua River, where colorful boats rock gently in the docks. In the evening, candles light the tables with a golden glow, and the air is soft and fragrant.

A pleasant waitress will probably recommend the fresh fish specials, and be sure to take the advice, for the fish is deliciously moist and tender. The mahi mahi is broiled to perfection, and the fresh ahi stuffed with crab ($11.25) is well seasoned and flavorful. The fresh ono with marina sauce ($10.75) is juicy, tender, and flaky, a generous portion of 2 large slices. A local favorite, the hot lobster salad ($4.95) is a true house specialty, a small casserole of lobster chopped with celery and mayonnaise and baked till both creamy and crispy—a much more satisfying appetizer than the rather thin clam chowder ($1.50) or the onion soup ($1) an overly salty version not unlike Liptons. Another wonderful entree is the local slipper lobster, a sweet and tender 6 oz tail served with a filet of fresh ono ($16) and accompanied with small cups of both teriyaki sauce and drawn butter.

The menu features no fewer than 41 entrees, with 8 under $6. Steaks start at $10.95, and dinner includes rolls, rice or potato, a salad which can charitably be described as small, and a vegetable, in our case 1/3 an ear of corn resting on a bed of shredded lettuce with an orchid atop an envelope of catsup! The hot, crispy french fries are considerably better than the somewhat greasy fried rice, although even that's not too bad if you flavor it with some of the kitchen's delicious teriyaki sauce.

When we took the children, we were able to sample more of the menu. The kids preferred the fried chicken ($4.30) to the relatively dry teriyaki chicken, but they loved the teriyaki sauce on the side for dipping! The roast beef ($12.95) was a bit mealy though of good size. The kitchen does best with fresh fish!

To keep prices this reasonable, the Marina cuts a few corners, but they're the kind no one really misses if you catch the spirit of the place. The pleasantness of the setting more than compensates for paper napkins and placemats. The salad dressing may not be quite enough for the salad which is not quite enough for the plate, but on the other hand, the rolls with whipped butter are light and fluffy and smell of the oven! If the salad dressing appears in a paper pill cup and the parmesan cheese in the kind of small envelope Lipton's uses for tea bags, just smile, for you can feed the whole family for less than you will believe possible. Prices are reasonable, portions generous, and children can chose from ten dinners for about $2 less than adult prices, which are reasonable to begin with. The 11 wines on the list are not very exciting, but there is a chardonnay by "Ernest and Julio" for only $10. Don't pass up the homemade coconut or macadamia nut pies ($1.50).

Dinner at the Wailua Marina will not cost you very much, but you'll come away well fed and well satisfied, with a pleasant memory of dining by candlelight, with the fragrance of flowers in the evening breeze and the lights on the river winking as the dusk deepens into night.

For breakfast, you can sit out by the boats and enjoy tasty eggs benedict ($4.50), delicious corned beef hash ($4) or bacon and eggs ($3.75). It's hot, fast, and filling—perfect for those mornings when you're on the way to the airport and need every ounce of strength to get those bags through the agriculture inspection without misplacing anything—or anybody!

On Rt 56 in Wailua. 8:30 am–9 pm daily. 822-4311 for reservations and free shuttle from Wailua area hotels and condos. Coffee/Sanka $.75. House wine: William Wycliff $4/$8.

Waipouli Deli & Restaurant

Does this sound familiar? Your body clock is off. You're fully awake—and starving—3 hours early. You'll never make it till lunch, but you want to spend the morning on the beach and not in some dark, air-conditioned restaurant with poky service!

Well, the Waipouli Deli is for you! Generous portions of tasty food coupled with speedy delivery and unbeatable prices have made the Waipouli Deli a favorite spot on the east coast for local families and increasing numbers of tourists. In fact, although in the past you had to wait for a table no matter when you arrived (there were, after all, only 6 tables), the hard working Japanese owner has moved her shop to larger, more comfortable quarters to accommodate the growing clientele.

Larger it is, but it still looks like formica city, so don't go expecting orchids on the table! But though short on atmosphere, it's got a "breakfast special" deserving of the name. For $1.99, you get an egg cooked as you like it, two slices of bacon, and two pancakes—perfect for hungry children, not to mention adults. Eggs are expertly cooked, side meats not overly fatty, and pancakes light. On the lunch and dinner menus, there are lots of bargains in American and Oriental food served luncheonette style.

Service is fast, efficient, and very friendly. Children receive smiles, crackers, and once even a pencil and paper for doodling. We were in and out and on our way in less than an hour! If you want to save money and be well fed before the morning slips away from you, this is your place!

On Rt 56 in the Waipouli Town Plaza, behind McDonald's.
Open 7:30 am-9:30 pm daily. 822-9311 for take-out orders.

Fast Foods

It still seems odd to see a McDonald's golden arch on this remote island paradise, but in both Lihue and Kapa'a you can close you eyes as you bite down on a Big Mac and feel like you've never left home. In addition to national chains like Pizza Hut, Burger King, and Taco Bell, some local operations offer fast food service at inexpensive prices. A favorite spot with the kids is **Mustard's Last Stand**, just to the west of Poipu, at the junction of Rt 50 and Rt 530, which seems to have been designed with kids in mind. Hot dogs ($2.95 or $2.25 under 12), are the house specialty, along with sausages, and quarter-pound hamburgers ($3.25). You can choose from no fewer than 20 condiments, including 5 mustards, 3 cheeses, 3 kinds of onions, guacamole, salsa, and sauerkraut. The hot dogs are excellent, according to our 9-year-old connoisseur Mikey: juicy, tasty and soft all around. While the kids are busy chewing, adults can visit a gift shop with a wide selection of shell necklaces and souvenirs at rock-bottom prices. After lunch, kids can have a wonderful time at the "Geckoland Mini Golfpark" next door and putt through nine holes representing miniature Kauaian landmarks such as "Waimea Canyon," "Sleeping Giant" and the "Tree Tunnel." It's the best dollar you'll ever spend! (9 am -7 pm daily).

For an inexpensive (around $3) "plate lunch", try the lunch counters at the **Big Save** Markets, or the **Dairy Queen** in Lihue, where you can get miso soup and a salad with an entree like boiled akule fish that, according to one reader, "has to be tasted to be appreciated." **Kauai Chop Suey** offers a "special plate"($4) which is almost enough to feed two, as does **Barbecue Inn.** At **Ho's Garden** in Lihue, $3 buys a large mound of crisp cooked vegetable chop suey, rice and Chinese meat balls. In Kapa'a, try **Dragon Inn** or **Restaurant Shiroma**.

On the eastern shore, **Ono Family Restaurant** and the **Waipouli Delicatessan and Restaurant** in Kapa'a offer a bargain priced children's hamburger platter which includes beverage. In Kilauea, **Jacques's Bakery** on Oka Street serves croissant sandwiches as well as light as a feather pastries on 5 tiny tables on a lanai adjacent to his ovens. The fragrance is heavenly. For breakfast, try coconut danish pastries! The bakery opens at 6:30 am! (828-1393). On the south shore, **Brennecke's Snack Shop** can whip up delicious hamburgers and sandwiches. Just cross the street and picnic at Poipu Beach Park!

North Shore Restaurants

Bali Hai

Imagine dining as the sunset paints the sky all gold and orange above the magnificent angles of the dark and mysterious mountains, turning the ocean almost purple in Hanalei Bay. Sip a cocktail while the cool evening breeze, fragrant with tropical flowers, touches your skin like silk. At the Bali Hai Restaurant, you can find the Kauai of your imagination, the dream of an island paradise that haunts you in the dead of winter.

The dining experience could not be more relaxing, with the food brought at a leisurely pace by polite waiters and served on large, elegantly appointed tables. Open to the air on three sides, the dining room has high ceilings, hung with brilliantly colored tapestries, and a two-tiered arrangement of tables which makes the room spacious and, even when full, remarkably quiet. As we lingered over coffee to watch a sudden shower fill the air with shining drops, we felt more at peace than when we arrived.

All the ingredients for a fantastic restaurant, one would think. But perhaps some *kapuna* haunts the kitchen, for in more than ten years of dining at Bali Hai, we have always found it difficult to find something good to eat while we occupied a table and enjoyed the sunset.

In fact, almost each time we have visited this restaurant, we have found a new chef or a new menu, and we have marveled again at how so many could fail with so spectacular a dining room!

The restaurant in its newest incarnation opened in October, 1986, and the dining experience has improved again with the introduction of a new menu in summer, 1988. About a dozen entrees are priced from $13.50 (teriyaki chicken) accompanied by soup or salad, a vegetable, and rice or potatoes. Still on the menu, despite all the management and ownership changes during the last ten years, is salmon in crust, which we have come to regard as an old friend, though now priced at a whopping $19.95. The wine list, which used to be both small and expensive, is now small but reasonably priced, with some good choices for less than $20, including a Silverado Sauvignon Blanc for $15 and a Robert Mondavi Fume Blanc for $18.

The seafood chowder was generous with fish and shrimps although bland, and the dinner salad was attractive and of reasonable size. The vegetable tempura appetizer ($6.75), though huge and well-mixed, could have been crispier. Entrees proved as variable as ever! The New York steak ($17.25) was marred by some gristle, and the filet mignon ($17.50), though tender, lacked character. A new selection, Hawaiian curry with shrimp ($17) or chicken ($14.25) looked attractive with grated fresh coconut and mango chutney and other condiments and was tasty, although the waiter at first tried to serve it with the house rice pilaf because the kitchen was temporarily out of white rice! The fresh ono ($18.50), which we took the precaution of ordering plainly sauteed, was perfectly cooked and delicious, by far the best dish.

We've had better luck at lunch. The lunch chef cooks an excellent hamburger, crisp on the outside, moist and juicy inside, and just the right size (1/3 pound) for the toasted sesame bun as well as for the price ($5.75). The teriyaki version came with delicious sauce on the side. Clam chowder ($2.25) was lightly creamy and delicately seasoned, full of clams and celery. The green salad ($2.25) was well worth the modest price, attractively served with cucumber, tomatoes and cauliflower on a glass plate, served with fresh Jacques's bread and butter. When not enough slices came for all our children, the helpful waitress Carmen brought extras at no charge. She even brought catsup in seven tiny individual serving cups! Sandwiches arrive with lots of hot, tasty, crispy french fries, which taste terrific with the au jus served with the delicious french dip sandwich. The crispy fried chicken in a basket ($6.50) was a big hit with the little ones, and enough for two to share, golden delicious and not greasy, a breast, leg, and thigh that disappeared to the last crumb. Service had the friendliness of grandma's kitchen, which made the lunch a great success with everyone, particularly the parents of all the children whose mouths were so busy chewing.

Bali Hai has a wonderfully romantic ambiance and unmatchable view. Even if the food were terrible, it would still be worth the price of admission. But meals are adequate if you don't ask the kitchen to prepare anything fancy. Think twice, however, about coming after sunset, when all you can see is the tennis courts lit for night games! Time your dinner for just before sunset, avoid all sauces, stick to the steak and fresh fish, and hope for the best!

When making reservations, ask to speak directly with the maitre de; that way you can avoid arriving at the restaurant to find no record of your call. Even if that should happen, do not despair. You can discover, as we did, a wonderful walk to a new lookout point for the sunset. Head towards the cliff along the sidewalk between the tennis courts. From path's end, you can look down at Hanalei Bay, sparkling with beads of light and turning dark purple as the sun descends. A sailboat cuts silently across the water, the sails filling with the breezes which brush your face and fill your head with the fragrance of evening flowers. The cliffs are like dark velvet, their sharp craggy edges blended by the sun's magic into soft purples and deep blues. The gold and orange sun slowly sinks towards the water, shining more brightly with each second, until flattened by the sea into a disk that shrinks to nothing before your eyes. A golden glow remains, burnishing the clouds, polishing the water, then slowly fades into a darkening dusk.

In Princeville. Reservations: 826-7670. Credit cards. House wine: Inglenook ($9). Coffee: $1. Children's entrees (steak, chicken, mahi mahi) $8.75. Dinner 5:30-10 pm.

Beamreach

In this small, unpretentious restaurant tucked away in the Pali Ke Kua condominium at Princeville, you can find the most superb filet mignon the island has to offer. A full two inches thick, this 12 oz steak is perfectly cut and perfectly cooked, at once tender and crisp, juicy and flavorful—a steak worth writing a postcard home about!

The secret is the finest Wichita beef flown in fresh twice, even three times a week. But prices in Wichita have been creeping up, and the Beamreach has faced the difficult choice between cutting corners and raising prices. They have wisely chosen not to compromise quality or to remove from the meal the features, like the family-style salad bowl and baked potato, that have always made the Beamreach special. The result has been, however, an sizeable jump in dinner prices. In our opinion, it's still worth it, even though $19.95 is top dollar for a steak dinner on Kauai.

The menu also features some some reasonably priced dinner choices too, like an outstanding chopped sirloin, an enormous 11 oz portion as tasty as it is generous, for only $10.95, or the boneless teriyaki chicken breasts for $12.95. For $8.95, you can have chili. But the real reason to come to Beamreach is the steaks, and they are nothing short of spectacular, particularly if cooked with a teriyaki sauce that enhances but does not smother its flavor. Unlike many restaurants, Beamreach manages to excel in both steak and fresh fish, for the fresh mahi mahi ($19.50) has the color, taste and flaking texture of magical timing. The fresh ahi and the fresh ono have also been perfectly cooked despite the thickness of the generous filets. Lobster tail is another excellent choice, broiled crisp and at the same time moist and tender. The portion is enormous, but whatever's left will make a great lunch the next day, or you can order a half portion (a single tail) instead.

Entrees are accompanied by rice or a full-size, delicious baked potato, as well as warm cracked-wheat and honey bread. While at many other restaurants, we have watched the salad shrink as produce prices have grown over the years, at the Beamreach you can count on salad being as fine as every part of your meal. You'll find fresh tomatoes and papaya and sprouts as well as homemade croutons in the enormous silver bowl, topped with excellent dressings, including a fine creamy Italian. Although dinner portions will satisfy the hungriest appetite, the onion soup ($3) is tasty and the beef vegetable soup outstandingly rich, spiced with flair and served piping hot. The ahi sashimi is wonderful, an enormous portion of thin and fragrant slices attractively arranged on a bed of shredded cabbage. Or try the cajun shrimp cocktail ($8.50) with very tender shrimp and spicy cajun sauce. The wine list is small but well selected, with half the sixteen choices $18 or less, including a Guenoc Sauvignon Blanc for $16, but be sure to try the house

specialty, absolutely sensational strawberry daiquiris. Finish off the meal with ice cream sundaes of generous scoops of Haagen Dazs or Meadow Gold, topped with a mountain of whipped cream ($3).

The service is as wonderful as the cooking, and the owner works even harder than her staff, bustling around from table to table to make sure that all her diners are happy. Everyone is friendly, and children are given a full dinner at a good price, not surprising since the owner's children personally selected the entrees: hot dog ($5.50), chicken ($6.95), and 5 oz filet ($6.95).

'Beamreach,' as the menu explains, refers to sailing before the swiftest wind, and the restaurant cues its decor to this nautical theme. The dining room is lovely in an understated way, with captain's chairs and polished wood tables lit romantically with candles. Regrettably the dining room lacks an ocean view—the only water you can see is in the apartment swimming pool. Come instead for great beef and the relaxed, intimate ambiance, and watch spectacular sunsets from the grounds outside before dinner.

In Princeville. Reservations necessary. 826-9131. Children's dinners ($4.50-10.50). Credit Cards. House wine: CK Mondavi $8.95/4.95.

Casa di Amici

It's an out of the way spot for an Italian restaurant—even on Kauai. You'll find Casa di Amici in the middle of sugar cane fields and papaya groves, on the back streets of Kilauea, a former sugar plantation town which still seems closer to Kauai's past than its present. Yet this dining room would be attractive anywhere—with fresh grey and white paint, a bright red tin roof, and sliding glass doors that open to evening breezes. In the candlelight, the dark green tables, rimmed with tan and colorful with red ginger blossoms, look romantic, and the rather spare decor has a charm all its own.

The menu offers something for everyone no matter how hungry. Seven pastas come in 'light or full' portions ($8 or $11), and can be served with your choice of five sauces, so pasta can either begin or end your meal, depending on your appetite. Four of the eleven veal, fish, and chicken entrees have the same price structure, and even the light portion is a generous size. You can choose from more than fifty Italian wines, with many less than $20, and the staff is well-informed about the selections.

The dining room operation—ambiance, menu, and service—is excellent . A new chef, imported from New Orleans, is improving the kitchen as well. The minestrone ($3.50) for example, is a richer, more interesting soup, with a rich tomato broth, colorful with carrots and still crunchy bell peppers and served in a tall crock to keep it hot. The small antipasto is generous for the modest price ($5). Cannelloni ($8/appetizer), two thin and elegant crepes, is presented with a deliciously light cream sauce as well as a pungent tomato sauce. The pasta is cooked *al dente* and served with a sauce with both character and flair.

Although veal scallopini ($10/light portion) was disappointingly bitter, the fresh ono ($19), an enormous filet, was very tender, with a taste remarkably like lobster. Fresh baked bread comes from the bakery next door (The Bread Also Rises), and entrees are served with rice and zucchini, unfortunately so garlicky that the taste out-lasted even an ice cream dessert.

Casa di Amici has no children's menu, and so at the minimum a child's bowl of spaghetti with meat balls will cost $8, and a coke will be $1 more. Families might try Casa Di Amici for lunch instead, for the lunch menu has a good selection of reasonably priced sand-wiches and salads, lunch plates and "authentic East Coast subma-rines" on homemade bread.

Kauai has few Italian restaurants, and none with as pretty a setting as this one. As the name suggests, Casa di Amici is a friendly place, and you really want the restaurant to succeed, although it has not yet achieved a distinctive cuisine. Give it a try, order the 'light' portions and hope for the best!

In Kong Lung Center, Kilauea, on the Lighthouse Road. Reservations 828-1388. Coffee $1.

Sunset Drive to Hanalei

If your accommodations are on the eastern shore, consider dinner in Hanalei, for the drive north as the sun begins to set is an experience not to be missed! Check the paper for the exact time of sunset, which may be earlier than you expect because the state of Hawaii never changes to daylight savings time. Plan to reach Hanalei about ten minutes before sunset so that you have time to park and ready your camera and are assured a spectacular drive north.

As you begin the drive, hundreds of clouds, already tinged with peach and gold, float in an azure sky above a shimmering sea. Rt 56 winds through the countryside and along the coast, with fields of sugar cane turning silver, and the colors of land and sky changing almost mile by mile as the declining sun deepens the greens and blues and touches everything with shades of pink and gold. At Kilauea, where the road curves to the west, a line of tall, graceful Norfolk pines stands starkly silhouetted against the blazing sky. Even the grasses, their feathery tops waving gently in the evening breeze, are touched with pink, and the cattle grazing in the field seem positioned by an artist's hand. Near Princeville, the clouds, luminous with reflected golds and pinks, seem enormous, dwarfing the cliffs, whose great jagged peaks have turned an astonishing purple.

We never tire of this drive, as each sunset is different—the gleaming expanse of ocean, the sharply angled mountains, the masses of clouds are blended each night by the sun's magic into a composition of colors that will never occur again in exactly the same way. One night the sun's descent may be screened by great masses of clouds rimmed with gold and glowing tangerine against the deep purple mountains and the shimmering blue gray sea. Another time the sun may almost blind you with its blazing, fiery gold, suffusing nearby clouds with impossible shades of orange and pink and brushing distant clouds with peach. Or, one evening the clouds may be so thick that the setting sun is apparent only in delicate touches of apricot on the clouds hovering over the sea, muted purples on the mountains, and the silver sheen on the surface of the sea. As the seasons change, so does the angle of the sun, gilding the landscape with new patterns of light and color.

In fact, as we discovered last summer, a sunset in the rain is the most astonishing of all, for it excites the imagination with impossible combinations. The tops of the mountains are shrouded with gray, yet above the sea, the sky is brilliant with color, with sunny clouds stretching along the horizon, their grey shapes rimmed with pink light

from the setting sun. As dark showers move across the horizon like 'legs of the rain,' blurring the line between ocean and sky, the sun's vivid orange is turning the water purple and the clouds violet. The sun descends into stormy clouds moving slowly toward it, and, as the last light fades, dark clouds hovering above the cliffs slowly creep across the mountains, and the world turns slowly still and dark.

If the clouds are not too thick, there are several places at Hanalei to enjoy the dramatic moment when the shining disk of sun slips silently into the sea. Less than a mile past the entrance to Princeville, you can park at a scenic overlook on Rt 56 and see most of Hanalei Bay's western side. But you have to contend with the distractions of traffic and car radios as well as the conversations of other sunset seekers ("Ralph! I *told* you we were going to miss it! We should have left earlier!") For a more panoramic view with greater privacy, enter Princeville and follow the signs to Pali Ke Kua, park in the lot, and enjoy the view discreetly from the lawn between the buildings.

The drive home after dinner is another sensuous experience of cool evening breezes you can almost taste as well as feel. As you drive south almost alone on the road, you can hear wonderful sounds—the chirping of crickets, the leaves rustling in the breeze—and see the different shades of darkness in the landscape, lit by the moon against an enormous star–filled sky and the shimmering waves of the wide ocean beyond.

Charo's

As we've all discovered halfway into at least one movie or night club performance, the show is not always worth the price of admission. Looking at Charo's sleek interior, you expect a professional food operation, but what you find is high prices, uneven quality, and service so bumbling that you wonder just what business the waiter is really trying to break into.

A quick glance will show you a menu high on prices and short on choices. The only items costing less than $5 are soup or a small salad, and the only available hot dog is stuffed with cheese and wrapped with bacon ($5.25). Without a children's menu, a family can quickly run up a large tab on sandwiches and cokes alone. At dinner, these same burgers and salads will cost you about a dollar more unless you choose a full dinner, including salad, vegetable, and pasta or rice, priced from $15.95 (chicken) to $41.95 (broiled lobster tail). Now the management offers a nightly dinner "fiesta" show in hopes of attracting more customers, so if you want a quiet dinner, call ahead to find out who's singing!

As far as lunch is concerned, for the high price of admission, you do not get first-run entertainment. We have been served sandwiches and salads which have ranged from delicious to disgraceful. For example, the turkey and macadamia nut salad served in a pita pocket ($7.50) was pretty pedestrian, a small scoop that tasted a little like turkey, less like nuts, and mostly like mayonnaise. But when we tried the turkey salad served in a skinned papaya ($7.95), the addition of fruit made the salad taste much less salty, and even better, the platter was heaped with slices of honeydew, canteloup, watermelon, oranges, kiwi, bananas and grapes! The high-priced chicken teriyaki ($7.50), on the other hand was so soggy that no one could be talked into eating it. We had better luck with the hamburger, a third of a pound for $5.75, which was, however, overcooked despite our request that it be served "pink in the middle." The fresh ahi sandwich, though a reasonable portion for the price ($9.50), was flawed by a bitter taste from the grill, and served with overseasoned sliced zucchini and rice. The best dish was the chicken fingers ($5.95), five crispy breast strips which five-year-old Lauren was able to praise as highly as Burger King's.

Service can be as variable as the food. Once we waited (not so quietly) for a full 25 minutes in a restaurant two-thirds empty, while on another visit, our food was served quickly and efficiently. On our most recent visit, the waitress who served our children at a separate table brought their food faster and more cheerfully and served them regular–sized cokes ($1). Our waitress, who had all the personality of the ahi filet, served Lauren the giant–sized coke ($1.85) which was far too big for her tummy, not to mention her grip!

There are some redeeming features. The interior is attractively decorated in woodgrain bamboo and rattan, with greens in the upholstery and abundant ferns and hanging plants. What was once a dark, cavernous room has been opened with skylights and a shiny tile floor (you may even need sunglasses for summertime lunches!). And some food we sampled was tasty. The clam chowder ($2.95/cup) was hot, creamy rather than thickened, flavored with pepper, and full of tender clams, and the cream of potato soup was a big hit with the small set. And it is hard to calculate the value that some people will place on the chance of seeing Charo, in the flesh, stroll through the restaurant and say hello.

We had high hopes for Charo's as a replacement of the Sand-groper, a legendary rip-off run by a cantankerous Australian who offered small portions at outrageous prices to diners with few other options after dark. The setting, tucked into the magnificent Haena coast looking out over the waves, is hard to equal. However, Charo's seems to have fallen victim to the curse of high overhead. Perhaps it is simply not possible to offer reasonably-priced food so far up the winding narrow road with its one-lane bridges, especially when many dinner customers don't want to drive those winding narrow roads after dark! Whatever the reason, this show gets low ratings! So if your children are sandy and hungry after a hard morning at the north shore beaches, and if they beg you to pull up in front Charo's, you might just close your ears, pass out the potato chips, and drive a few miles more for lunch at Tahiti Nui or Chuck's!

Adjacent to the Hanalei Colony Resort, Haena. Reservations 826-6422. Lunch 11:30 am-3 pm and dinner 5:30-10 pm daily.

Chuck's Steak House

People who live on Kauai seem to like Chuck's in Hanalei even though (or perhaps, even because) it looks more like a mainland restaurant than a tropical island hideaway. When you walk through the door, you could be in Chuck's in West Haven, Connecticut, one of nearly fifty Chuck's Steak Houses which have opened across the nation since the first Chuck's opened more than 20 years ago. Each is supposed to have the special identity that comes with individual ownership. But the name says it all. This is not Ernie's but Chuck's, and to our mind a chain is a chain is a chain. This happens to be a good chain, but don't expect a unique cuisine, or personalized, attentive service. For example, if you don't specifically request pacing the dinner, your entree will arrive when you've barely finished your salad. And don't expect distinctive decor. Fly fans hum on open-beamed ceilings, and candles glow on polished tables in dark booths, but two weeks after your visit you will probably not be able to remember many details of the interior, except that it was carpeted and comfortable. That is, unless you are seated on the porch, which seems to be a great deal cooler and more desirable until the mosquitoes attack!

Prices are reasonable and menu choices extensive. More than 25 entrees range from $11.50 (barbecued beef ribs) to $18.50 (11-13 oz prime rib), including 4 children's dinners from $6.95 (teriyaki chicken) to $10.95 (prime rib). Dinners include rice, warm bread and butter, and a visit to the salad bar, a modest affair of romaine and tomatoes, a few fresh vegetables and prepared salads, and fruits. Excellent dressings, including the best blue cheese we found, and fresh ground pepper save it from oblivion. Go early and take some homemade cracker bread to munch on with your cocktails or wine. There are not many choices on the wine list, but all are reasonable, with the most expensive a 1985 Sterling chardonnay for $23.

Over the years, we have found dinners at Chuck's to be reasonably priced and reliably well-prepared. Barbecued beef ribs are usually enormous, served with a flavorful sauce, and not overly fatty, though on a recent visit, two of the four ribs were less meaty than one would prefer. The New York steak (12 oz for $16.50) was excellent, very tender and juicy with great flavor and no gristle. The kitchen will prepare it with teriyaki sauce upon request.

Families might try Chuck's for lunch. Hamburgers ($5.75) are a third of a pound and delicious, and kids will like the hot dog ($2), which according to our nine-year-old Mikey, was crispy and tender and "soft all around." Our prime rib sandwich ($7.75), though not as well-trimmed as it might have been, was tasty, moist, and miraculously medium-rare, served with a sauce that made it come alive. Though the deep fryer was on the blink and we couldn't have french fries ($1 extra with sandwiches), a cheerful waitress brought us plates of chips on the house. Keep in mind that kids' sodas are priced from the bar ($1.25 each).

Lunches and dinners at Chuck's will be reasonably priced and probably reasonably good. Chuck's does not try to achieve anything spectacular or to create a unique cuisine. On the other hand, you don't get anything special either, in food or ambiance. Chuck's offers no views of Hanalei's magnificent mountains or valleys to paint a memory for dark winter evenings back home. Its reputation among local people may have something to do with that. Unlike many of us, who dream of vacationing on Kauai, perhaps they dream of vacationing in West Haven, Connecticut.

In Princeville Center, Hanalei. Reservations 826-6211. Credit cards. Coffee/brewed decaf $.75. House wine: Round Hill $8/$5. Lunch 11:30 am-2:30 m. Dinner 6 pm-11:30 pm daily.

Foong Wong

The drive north to Hanalei for dinner, we have always believed, is spectacular enough to be worth any meal, whatever the quality. That faith has been sorely tried by our dinners at Foong Wong, where despite generous portions, the dishes are bland bordering on tasteless. Wor wonton soup ($5.75), for example, arrives at your table in a gorgeous, steaming tureen packed with miniature corn ears, pork, shrimp, carrots, straw mushrooms, and won tons. But as far as flavor goes, you could be drinking water.

Another time we tried Foong Wong for lunch, and we brought the children along for a wider range of opinion. But the cooking was almost equally disappointing, the seasoning either non-existent or heavy on salt. The egg roll ($1.80), was in the words of our six-year old, "empty" and greasy. A better choice was the crisp gau gee, a portion of ten for $4.50. Of the plate lunches, which include fried rice or noodles, a few crispy won tons, and mixed vegetables, the chicken ($4.75) was rated "OK" by our babysitter, who then pushed it quietly to the side of her plate. Best was the saimin ($2.95), which the children devoured to the last noodle. The kitchen usually features a fresh catch, like a Pacific lobster or a local fish called minpori, stir fried in a sauce which tends toward the pasty and can be full of chunks of ginger too small to pick out and too large to ignore. Even the pan-fried cake noodle ($7.25), which we have enjoyed on past visits, was overly salty this time around, although it still looked lovely, the thin noodles crisp fried in a cake, cut into squares and garnished with broccoli, carrots and mushrooms.

There's nothing special about the setting. While clean and bright, Foong Wong looks rather like a cafeteria. Parquet floors, louvered windows, brown formica tables and red folding chairs provide the color scheme; the decor is a combination of plants, red Chinese lanterns, and a 7-Up clock. A bamboo fence, complete with a few branches and leaves, divides the restrooms from the rest of the dining room and complements the bamboo arch, lit with Christmas lights, over the entrance. Service is efficient, pleasant, extremely polite, and so quiet that older folks like to spend the afternoon sipping tea and reading novels to the hum of the fans, hopefully not disturbed by a group of boisterous short persons engaged in a vocal count of fried noodles in the interest of numerical equality.

At Foong Wong, you'll find the food at best inoffensive, and it's a shame, for the people are pleasant, it offers full bar service, and it's the only Chinese restaurant on the north shore. But if you have an uncontrollable yen for Chinese, and if your car has broken down in Hanalei, you might give serious thought to a can of Chun King!

In the Ching Young Shopping Center, Hanalei. 826-6996. Credit cards. Lunch 11 am-4 pm; dinner 5 pm-9 pm. Breakfast 6:30 am-11 am Tues-Sun.

Hanalei Dolphin

The Dolphin has always had the reputation of serving the finest seafood on the north shore. Service is friendly and leisurely in the softly lit dining room, slightly warm from the open grill in the rear. The decor is rustic, quaint without appearing contrived. Wooden shutters are raised to let in evening breezes, and lanterns glow pleasantly on polished table tops. Hope that the rock music tapes have been turned off so you can enjoy the sounds of the crickets!

The small restaurant is almost always crowded, but if you choose a weeknight and arrive around 7 pm, you shouldn't have a long wait. Even better, arrive earlier, leave your name with the hostess, and drive a few blocks to Hanalei Bay and watch the sunset. By the time you get back to the Dolphin, your table should be ready! The Dolphin, if you haven't already guessed, is a favorite destination for our spectacular sunset drives north from Wailua!

Over the past few years, if we have had an occasional disappointing dinner at the Dolphin, we have chalked it up to bad luck in the kitchen. According to our waiter, two and sometimes three chefs alternate during the week, and so the cooking inevitably varies. One night, both ono filets we ordered came out partially raw, an error easily corrected. On our most recent visit (Jeffrey was in the kitchen), the broiled fresh ono (a 12 oz filet for $18) was perfectly cooked— moist, tender, and flaky—cleanly broiled, with no taste of the grill. The ahi teriyaki ($18) is always a winner, and it remains one of the most delicious fish dinners on Kauai—juicy, tender, and full of spark. Dinners come with fresh hot bread from Jacques's bakery in Kilauea, and a big bowl of delicious green salad with cherry tomatoes, bean sprouts, and choice of oil and vinegar, or creamy garlic or Russian dressings. Prices range from $12 (chicken) to $20 (shrimp and steak), and for $8 you can have a "light dinner" of broccoli casserole or soup, salad, rice or french fries, and bread. The seafood chowder ($4.00), is creamy, hot, and full of fish and potatoes, and the steak fries are thick, hot, and crispy.

The wine list is very well-selected, with lots of choices in the moderate range, like a Mondavi Fume Blanc at $20. Even better, our bottle was presented in a bucket filled to the top with water and ice so that the wine was perfectly chilled. We were sad to discover that an old friend on the wine list—the bottle of Chateau Lafitte Rothschild, which survived Hurricane I'wa even when the roof did not —was no longer available for $200. Suddenly, we felt older.

The Dolphin is an expensive place to take a risk on uneven cooking. On the other hand, the setting is wonderful, the service is friendly, and the opportunity to see the sunset before eating is not to be missed. Take your chances, stick to basics, and warn the waiter that any overcooked fish will be thrown back, if not into the ocean, at least onto his tray!

On Rt 56 in Hanalei, just past Princeville and the bridge over the Hanalei River. No reservations. To see who's cooking, call 826-6113. Jeffrey usually cooks Fridays-Sundays. Children's dinners: chicken or steak ($7.00) shrimp ($8.50). House wine: Inglenook $7/$4. Coffee $.1.

Hanalei Shell House

The Shell House has the kind of bar where the bottles provide more than half the decor, with the rest contributed by a Lions Club sign, an antique rifle, and a painting of a mountain scene. And the bar is more than half the decor for the dining room, with the remainder contributed by leafy plants. The small dining room, which contains only eight tables, is also perched right on the street. In the days when you could count the number of cars traveling Rt 560 on your fingers, this location was a plus. Now you must expect the traffic noise to be dominant if not distracting.

Lunch will be expensive for a family. Children have to order adult portions, and sodas are priced as bar beverages at nearly $1 each. The menu features four different burgers, several sandwiches and salads, with the best deal the combination of clam chowder, the Shell House's specialty, and a sandwich for $5.75. The clam chowder ($1.95 for a cup; $3.95 for a bowl) is truly special, made with real cream, delicately flavored with rosemary, and chunky with clams and potatoes. Charbroiled hamburgers ($4.50) are juicy and tasty, although on more than one visit overcooked, even burnt on the outside. If this happens to you, simply send it back for a re-make! For the picky eaters in our family, the other sandwiches were even less reliable. Our daughter's quesadilla ($5.50) was too mushy and soggy for easy eating. The fresh ahi sandwich ($6.95) contained a thin steak, tasty but somewhat dry, accompanied with homemade tartar sauce. Sandwiches include steak fries, baked beans, or cole slaw, and some come with a tasty pasta salad which fortunately our five-year-old loved, for she ate every available tiny cup. The dinner menu contains many of the same selections, as well as steaks and seafood, priced from $8.95 (hamburger, soup, salad) to $18.95 (cajun blackened fish and salad).

Perhaps the best deal, and the best meal is the huge Shell House breakfast, which makes it a popular stop for the teenagers who work in the local tourist industry!

In Hanalei village. Breakfast and lunch daily 8 am-4 pm daily (Sunday Brunch 8-11:30 am). Dinner from 4:30 pm daily.

Lanai Restaurant

Live entertainment is becoming harder to find in restaurants on Kauai, particularly when combined with good food. At the Lanai Restaurant, soft Hawaiian melodies played on the guitar create just the right mood for watching the sun set over the golf course, turning the Hanalei cliffs purple and skimming the ocean with silver.

Inside, the restaurant is quiet and attractively decorated in greens and whites, with plants on the tables and candles flickering playfully in cool evening breezes. The menu features 11 entrees, from $13.95 (stir fry vegetables) to $19.95 (fresh fish), as well as several nightly specials. Dinners include soup or salad, vegetable, and rice or potato. On the wine list, you'll find most choices less than $20, including a 1986 David Bruce Chardonnay and a Sterling Fume Blanc for $18.

Service is polite and efficient, and the food is well prepared and sometimes imaginative, like a delicious chicken soup delicately flavored with ginger and lemon grass, and garnished with water chestnuts. On another visit, the fresh fish chowder was sensational, with generous chunks of ahi and ono in a soup that was creamy rather than thick and perfectly seasoned. Served piping hot along with a delicious round loaf of fresh sourdough, it was a wonderful way to start the meal. Or try the salad , which arrives in a large wooden bowl, colorful with carrots, radishes and whole scallions, and flavored with excellent dressing.

Though not very large, the menu offers chicken, fish, and beef in a variety of preparations. You can order fresh fish broiled, sauteed, or blackened New Orleans style. We prefer fresh fish cleanly sauteed—without the garlic or wine sauces that so often overwhelms the flavor—and the kitchen complied. We were very pleased with the generous portion of ono, cooked cleanly so that it was both tender and moist. The teriyaki chicken ($13.95) was another good choice, and so was the veal marsala, very tender in a sauce flavored with sauteed mushrooms. With the entrees came broiled potato slices seasoned with too much tarragon, and a vegetable, in our case sauteed fresh zucchini and yellow squash still bright and crunchy. If you stick to plain dishes and don't ask the kitchen for any fancy footwork, you can have a pleasant meal in a lovely, quiet setting at a reasonable price. And you can enjoy some excellent music. Check the schedule for who is playing, for entertainers alternate during the week except on Sundays, and request a table on the upper tier so that you look out to the mountains rather than into the swimming pool!

In Princeville. Credit cards. Reservations 826-6226.
Dinner 5-9:30 pm daily. Children's hamburger dinner $6.95 (under 12). House wine: William Wycliff $4.50/$8.95. Coffee: $1.

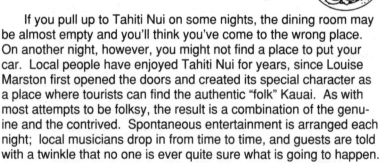

Tahiti Nui

If you pull up to Tahiti Nui on some nights, the dining room may be almost empty and you'll think you've come to the wrong place. On another night, however, you might not find a place to put your car. Local people have enjoyed Tahiti Nui for years, since Louise Marston first opened the doors and created its special character as a place where tourists can find the authentic "folk" Kauai. As with most attempts to be folksy, the result is a combination of the genuine and the contrived. Spontaneous entertainment is arranged each night; local musicians drop in from time to time, and guests are told with a twinkle that no one is ever quite sure what is going to happen.

The bar, not the dining room, is the real hub of Tahiti Nui. Decorated in what can only be described as early grass shack, the small, darkened lounge has touches of the genuinely unique (an inflated blowfish used as a lantern) as well as the genuinely corny (the portrait of the topless Tahitian perched over the cash register).

The bar is a favorite spot for local people to talk to old friends ov
generous drinks. For tourists, it's a great place to meet old timer_
and hear fascinating stories about the island. Even Tahiti Nui's
famous luaus (M,W,F $20/pp) are more like local talent shows than
the typical "Hawaiian" extravaganza. Entertainment is provided by
whoever happens by, usually local performers on their time off, as
well as the Maka family, playing ukeleles and a washtub with infec-
tious enjoyment and a group of lovely and graceful dancers. Even
guests occasionally join the entertainers.

On the other nights, Tahiti Nui is like any other restaurant, or
almost. Recent remodeling may have made the dining room more
attractive and modernized the tiny kitchen, where you used to be
able to watch the chef stir and chop and nibble and chat. But Tahiti
Nui is still in a class by itself. For what can you say about a place
where the carafe of house wine is the most expensive white wine on
the menu, if indeed there are any other wines on the menu that
night? Where the dinner menu features only six dinners, and one of
the choices is squid? Well, expect the unexpected. With an exotic
cocktail, you might sample some wonderful crisp won tons ($4.75)
served on a bed of lettuce and shredded carrot. Though last year's
dozen has shrunk to nine, the won tons have the light crunchiness
that only comes from being cooked to order. The chef last summer,
Jeff, seasons with flair and finesse. The tomato soup ($2) was
sensational, served piping hot in a chicken stock rather than cream
base, thick with zucchini and tomatoes and garnished with scallions.
The won ton soup, by comparison, was a little flat, though colorful
with green onions, mushrooms and grated carrot.

Dinners include a small salad, rice, and hot fresh garlic bread.
The New York steak, marinated in a subtle teriyaki sauce, was crisp
yet juicy and exceedingly tender, and a good size considering its
modest price ($12.95). An extra bonus, it came with a first-rate
baked potato. The fresh ono ($14.95) was moist, flaky, and flavored
with a delicious butter and wine sauce. Both were accompanied with
sauteed zucchini, onions and tomatoes. Your other menu choices
are calamari ($12.95), chicken curry ($10.95) freshwater prawns
($12.95) and pork ribs ($12.95). Finish off your meal with a slice of
excellent macadamia nut pie ($1.75).

Lunch is a gamble at Tahiti Nui. First, the restaurant may or may
not be open (Louise closes when business is slow), and even if
you're in luck, the kitchen may not have what is on the menu.
In fact, the kitchen may not have a chef at all, as happened on our
last two tries. This was a great disappointment to our children,

sandy and starving and not in the mood for compromise! They wanted the huge turkey sandwiches and the wonderful cooked-to-order hamburgers! They also remember the serendipity possible in a tiny restaurant, the time when the waitress served our family, which took up two tables, double baskets of hot, buttery garlic bread for the single order price ($1.75), or the time when the chef offered us all some soup, because she was about to cook up a fresh pot and needed to finish off the day's supply first! Because lunch at Tahiti Nui is such a family favorite, we hope Louise gets someone into the kitchen before our next vacation!

In the heart of Hanalei village, on Rt 56. Reservations 826-6277. Luau Mon. Wed. & Fri. nites at 7 pm. Credit cards. Coffee or sanka $.60. House wine: Paul Masson $7.50/$3.75.

Tropical Chicken Salad

Mix together chopped nuts, apple chunks, chicken chunks, diced celery and carrots in quantities you like, along with enough mayonnaise to blend. Add 1/2 to 1 tsp curry. Let stand about 1/2 hour.

Garnish with sliced bananas and chopped macadamic nuts. Serve on a bed of manoa lettuce. Dressing: blend 1/2 mashed ripe banana with 1/2 cup mayonnaise, salt, pepper and juice of 1/2 fresh lemon.

Flank Steak Lae Nani

Marinade: 1/4 cup honey or sugar, 1/3 cup hot water, 1/3 cup soy sauce, 2 tbsp oil, 1 clove garlic, 1 star anise or 1 thick slice fresh ginger.

Marinate at least 48 hours in the fridge, grill steak over coals or saute it in a pan. Slice across the grain in thin slices, angled about 45 degrees. The star anise, available dry in oriental grocery markets, gives the steak a unique, superb flavor, a delicate touch of licorice!

Cafe Zelo's Deli & Expresso Bar

Cafe Zelo's looks and tastes very much like California. The dining room shines in cheerful white, with green leafy plants hanging on rafters and colorful abstract paintings on whitewashed walls. Light blue formica tables and blond rattan chairs look clean and inviting, and behind the grey and white counter, a shining copper expresso machine presides over the proceedings, its image resplendent in the mirrored wall behind.

Cafe Zelo's offers an upscale pasta *cum* delicatessen menu, with most lunch items priced around $5 and most breakfast choices at around $4. In addition to pastas, salads and sandwiches, you'll find a variety of Lion brand coffees and steamed beverages as well as croissants and pastries. On the dismal afternoon when we arrived, the spinach lasagne was hot, moist and tasty, the spinach still green. Chicken fajitas sizzled cheerfully in the pan, with lots of celery, onions and carrots in a rather peppery sauce, alongside bowls of grated cheddar and sour cream. The roast beef sandwich, however, was thin on meat and heavy on lettuce and alfalfa sprouts.

Service was slow, primarily because we drew a waitress who seemed stuck in perpetual slow motion. Perhaps, like many things, she would have been less limp in the sunshine!

In the Princeville Shopping Center. Open daily 8 am-6 pm (3 pm on Sundays). 826-9700.

Exploring Kauai

Helicoptering Kauai

Many of the most beautiful places on Kauai are inaccessible by car. For this reason, a helicopter tour is an unforgettable way to see this spectacular island. As these tours have become increasingly popular, more companies have entered the market, and intense competition has developed, complete with discount coupons. Many people on the island feel that there is a wide variation in quality and safety, however. We have heard disquieting reports: some companies speed up tours in order to cut costs and squeeze in more paying customers; some are plagued with high turnover in pilots who may have sufficient flying hours to be licensed but limited experience over Kauai's unique terrain. In 1985, the Federal Aviation Administration took action against two of the largest companies for violations of proper maintenance and pilot training procedures, and at least one company is under investigation as we go to press.

With pilots from seventeen companies crowding the skies, safety is becoming an increasingly important issue, and you should do your homework carefully before making a choice. The cheapest tour is not necessarily the safest, or even the best value! First, find out whether the company is operating under a certificate issued by the Federal Aviation Administration under Part 135 of Federal Aviation Regulations. In order to maintain a certificate of this type, the company must follow a more rigorous (thus more expensive) maintenance program, and its pilots must pass annual flight tests not required of companies operating under Part 91 of Federal Aviation Regulations. At our last count, only about a dozen of the companies offering commercial tours on Kauai had been issued Part 135 operating certificates by the FAA, and these certificates can be revoked or suspended from time to time for violations. If the FAA has issued this certificate, it must be displayed in the company's office. Ask to see it! Or check ahead of time by phoning the Federal Aviation Administration in Honolulu between 7:30 am and 4 pm Monday through Friday at (808) 836-0615. Ask to speak to an Operations Inspector and inquire whether the companies you are considering are currently

certificated under Part 135 of Federal Aviation Regulations. The distinction between Part 135 and Part 91 operators can tell you about the standards a company operates under, although this information is no guarantee of a company's performance when you're in the aircraft.

The second question to ask is exactly how long the tour is. Actual in-flight time for the around the island tour should be no less than 55 minutes, or Kauai will appear to whiz past your window. Even a 55-minute tour limits the opportunities to explore up close the more remote terrain inside the island's perimeter, or to take satisfying pictures. But don't take the company's word for it. Ask for the daily flight schedule, subtract 5 minutes for re-fueling between flights, and draw your own conclusions! For all these reasons, we continue to consider Jack Harter the person to fly with on Kauai. He flies every flight himself, and he is the most experienced pilot around, having offered the first air tour on Kauai more than 25 years ago. His flights are at least an hour and a half, the best value for your money, and his pace is slow enough for you to take a good look at the island's remote terrain. But there's only one Jack Harter, and he flies only three tours a day. So if you're a planner, write ahead to Jack Harter Helicopters, PO Box 306, Lihue HI 96766 because, if you wait till you're on the island, chances are you won't get on.

Otherwise, we recommend interviewing several companies by asking specific questions and listening carefully to the answers before making your choice. Ask who your pilot will be, and how many hours he has had flying over Kauai. Not every pilot who qualifies for a helicopter license has had extensive experience with Kauai's wilderness terrain. You also have a right to know whether your pilot has been involved in any accidents during the past three years. Beware of companies which are reluctant to provide specific answers, or which say they "can't be sure" who will be piloting your flight. Call another company! And don't take at face value the advertisements which claim that the owner is the "operator." Any owner can "operate" his company without being the pilot for every flight. That may be true of some flights—from one a day to one a month—but very possibly not true of your flight!

One first-rate owner-pilot is Will Squyres, widely respected for his good judgment and meticulous maintenance. Will's tour is longer than most, lasting a little more than an hour, and he offers a lively commentary on Kauai's colorful past and present. Experienced and affable, Will mixes wit with skill as he guides his craft in and out and over ridges and cliffs for dramatic views, explaining with obvious love how and why his helicopter can move the way it does. His tour is not only exciting, but fun. He flies only three days a week, however, so if you want to fly with Will himself, rather than his asistant pilot, be sure to call in advance to schedule your tour.

There is no one like Jack Harter, however, and most of the other pilots on Kauai will tell you that—no one who knows as much about Kauai, and no one who can pilot his craft so magically, as smoothly as a dandelion seed, in almost any weather. A local legend, Jack is the pilot most often called upon for help in emergencies. Part of what makes him so special is that for Jack, helicoptering is more than just a business, and several Division of Forestry botanists doing research in a remote rainforest, or telephone workers repairing cables on an isolated mountain top, can tell stories of receiving a miraculous "drop" of pizza, pot roast, and beer from a helicopter appearing out of nowhere.

Jack's enormous knowledge is enough to make his tour memorable. Throughout the flight, he talks non-stop about the island he clearly loves, telling its legends and history, describing its plants and animals, reflecting on its politics and problems, and arguing the need for conservation and planned development.

Kauai is breathtakingly beautiful from the air, and Jack turns hs craft from side to side to make sure that each passenger with a camera gets an opportunity for the "great shots" that can happen at almost any moment. The back seats next to windows which open are best for photographing, and in the co-pilot's seat, you look down through the glass under your feet as if you were floating in a bubble.

And what you see is beyond your fantasies—a mountain goat poised for an instant in a ravine, a white bird gliding against the dark green cliffs, a sudden rainbow in the mist, incredible, tower-like mountains of pink and brown in the Waimea "Grand Canyon," a glistening waterfall hanging like a slender silver ribbon through trees and rocks, a curve of pure white sand at the base of the purple and gold Na Pali cliffs, a spray of shining white foam bursting upon the rocky coast. Then, like the unveiling of the island's final mystery, the entrance into the very center of Mt Waialeale's crater, where in the dimly lit mists of the rainiest place on the earth, waterfalls are born from ever falling showers. You have journeyed to the very heart of the island, the place of its own birth from the volcano's eruption centuries ago. From your hotel room, you would never have believed that all this splendor existed, and your only regret will be that you didn't take more film.

It's so special, you yearn to go up again. Even the second time, the tour is exhilarating. In fact, with a better sense of the island's geography, you are more sensitive to details too easily missed when you are overcome by the majesty of the scene for the first time. Perhaps you'll see some of the amazing irrigation canals and tunnels carved into the mountains a century ago to bring water to the sugar cane fields below. Or, on some remote and rocky precipice, a banana plant somehow thriving, all the more incredible because banana plants cannot grow from seed and must have somehow been planted there by the Hawaiians—generations before the arrival of helicopters! If you inform the office that you've been up with Jack before, he will try to modify the tour to show you some new hidden places. Kauai will astonish you with terrain like an America in miniature, with rolling hills and valleys on the east coast and majestic mountains on the west. The island has a flat, dry southland as well as a forested wilderness to the north, and, on the west coast, wide sandy beaches where the setting sun paints the sky with gold before slipping silently into the enormous sea. There is even a "Grand Canyon" on a small scale, where pink and purple cliffs, etched by centuries of wind and rain into giant towers, seem like remnants of a lost civilization. So much variety is amazing on an island only 30 miles in diameter!

Because of the expense of the tour, we worried about picking the "perfect day." That proved unnecessary. We began on what seemed in Lihue to be only a partly sunny day, but once in the air, we realized that the clouds would be above us rather than in our way and even enhanced the island's beauty with changing patterns of light. If the weather is too poor for a satisfying flight, Jack will cancel the trip. And even if you have already set out and he decides it is wiser to return, he will refund your money. Looking at our slides and video tapes back home almost brings back the magic of that hour, when we seemed suspended in a horizon so vast as to seem limitless, and any effort to confine it within camera range was impossible. It is always the best day of the trip!

Boat Tours

Ten years ago, the spectacular cliffs of the Na Pali coast were off limits to visitors—unless they dared to hike on narrow and slippery trails, or helicoptered over the steep and jagged ridges at a respectful distance. This stark wilderness which bands the island's northwest corner is still almost completely inaccessible, although today, coastal boat tours are becoming an increasingly popular way to see at least some of these amazing cliffs up close. In fact, on a clear summer's day it's hard to leave Hanalei Bay without seeing a half dozen rubber zodiacs and an assortment of large and small launches and catamarans loaded with tourists either on their way out or coming back in!

At about half the price of a helicopter tour, boat tours are a more affordable alternative and, to some people, a lot more fun. Boats offer rough and ready adventure, particularly the inflatable rubber "zodiacs" originally made popular for white water river rafting. In a calm ocean, the zodiacs can carry passengers right up to touching distance of the incredible cliffs, so close you can see water from mountain springs trickle through the rocky ridges and drop in shining ribbons to the sea. You can trace the patterns made over centuries by mineral deposits, or chronicle the island's history in lines of lava. You can explore caves etched into the cliffs, watch waterfalls sparkle in the sunshine, and marvel at how tenaciously plants and trees can cling to inhospitable rock. Dolphins may leap in arcs around you, so friendly they seem to be seeking companions in these strange looking black boats decked with brightly colored tourists.

Spectacular and romantic, boat tours are also big business. More than thirty companies are licensed on Kauai, offering half and full-day tours costing upwards of $65 per person. Because these companies compete so aggressively, many people on Kauai worry about safety: some companies run tours in marginal weather; others cram their boats to the maximum.

As a general rule, tours are the safest from May until October when the ocean is usually flat off the Na Pali coast. But the weather becomes much more unpredictable after winter storms begin in late October, and winter surf can reach twenty feet in Hanalei Bay. At that time of year sailboats and small craft are actually moved out of Hanalei to more protected Nawiliwili harbor on the island's southeastern leeward shore. Even after the small craft leave Hanalei for the winter, however, some companies still offer Na Pali coast boat tours. And although the companies will assure you that they run Na Pali tours only in safe weather, part of what makes the north shore so dangerous in winter is the unpredictability of the winds and the ocean swell. Winds can shift in twenty minutes, and so predicting surf conditions for up to six hours ahead can be tricky business!

Even on the best of summer days, the trip out along the Na Pali coast is a lot smoother than the return trip, when you ride into the wind and the water is more choppy. If the captain tells you the trip will be "wet and wild," he means the boat will be rolling up and down the swells, smacking into them with bursts of spray, definitely not a good idea for someone with a bad back! The return trip has been described as "riding the bull," and some adventurers even choose to sit astride the boat's inflated sides, although dangling legs are fair game for any Portuguese men o' war who happen to be floating by.

Because winter weather can be so chancy, you should pay careful attention to the company's "cancellation policy." Most companies will charge you between 20% and 50% of the tour price if you cancel less than 24 hours in advance, and the company can collect this cancellation charge because they will probably take down your credit card number as a way of confirming your reservation when you make it. Be forewarned: this policy leaves you little option if you don't feel comfortable with the look of the sky or the ocean on the morning of your tour. You may end up being charged if the company decides to send out the boats, even if your own assessment of the weather has made you decide not to be on board!

Boat traffic is another safety problem. You can see the results at Tunnels Beach, for example, long a favorite spot for north shore snorkeling. Because it's also the departure point for Captain Zodiac boat tours, you have to watch out for the boats as well as the fish when you're in the water! Boats and people have to share the only sandy channel out into the reef, and sometimes boat personnel can be overzealous in trying to keep swimmers out of the channel when boats are coming in or going out. Just remember: people, not boats, have the right of way!

All other boat company tours leave from the bank of the Hanalei Stream where it empties into Hanalei Bay. The sheer number of tours makes the departure point look like the first day of summer camp, so don't expect a lot of personal attention. The chiefs of each company bustle about, lists in hand, marshalling their groups, calling roll, and assigning people to boats which are pulled in for boarding like waiting schoolbuses, a time—consuming process, and annoying if you have to wait for the inevitable stragglers to show up.

Once out of Hanalei Bay, the view of the coast is spectacular, from the Haena reefs to Ke'e Beach, and then beyond to the cliffs where you and the porpoises share the same view of the craggy rock formations, the caves etched into sheer cliff, and the magnificent colors of sea and sky, the changing light of sun and shadow. When you ride into the caves, you plunge into a cold, wet world where the water sloshes eerily against the rocks, making you grateful to return to sunlight again. In one cave, the sunlight streams in through a giant hole in the ceiling, and a waterfall plunges in shining streams of sparkling drops.

At Hanako'a, the landscape changes from the dark, rich green of Hanalei to the reds and browns of the west, where vegetation is more sparse. While rainfall at Ke'e Beach measures nearly 125 inches a year, at Polihale on the westernmost end of the cliffs, it is only 20 inches.

The tour usually includes a stop for snorkeling and snacking, usually at Nu'alolo Kai, a calm spot with a protective reef where you can see hundreds of colorful fish. If you don't enjoy snorkeling, however, or if the weather is is not cooperative, this stop is a waste of time. If it's sunny, beware a burn! Bring plenty of sunscreen, and perhaps a hat and sunglasses to protect against the glare. For the return trip, which will be much more choppy, you might bring towels and dry clothes in a plastic bag. As the boat slaps head on into the waves, the salt spray can douse everything in the boat, including you and your camera! Some companies offer a power cruiser ride back, which is certainly more comfortable, but as far as your view of the cliffs goes, it's like looking through the window of a tour bus! And despite the relative protection from the swell, some travelers still get seasick.

Different craft will give you a different ride and a different experience of the coast line. Power boats are more comfortable than the rubber zodiacs, but they cannot hug the cliffs like the zodiacs, and the larger ones can't go into the caves. A compromise may be the small power catamarans, which are agile enough to go into the larger caves, and yet able to cut through the swell rather than riding up and over it. In winter months, you might consider a boat tour on the south shore, which may be less spectacular but is also safer and more comfortable.

Before you choose your tour, call several companies. Find out about the expected weather and surf conditions, and ask about the company's cancellation policy. You can also check with Marine Weather at 245-3564. Compare the coast guard-rated capacity of the craft with the number of passengers the company usually takes on board, keeping in mind that the more crowded the boat, the less comfortable you may be. Ask about your captain's experience; although every captain has to be coast guard licensed, some have more experience than others! And look carefully at discount coupons. One company, for example, offered a coupon for a $30 discount off a list price of $90. However, the same tour averaged about $65 at activity centers around the island, and just about no one ever paid the list price! And ask if you can save money by booking directly with the company rather than through an agent.

Museums and Special Tours

The story of Kauai is in many ways the story of the sugar plantations which shaped the island's multi-ethnic culture as much as its agriculture and economy, For this reason, a visit to the **Grove Farm Homestead** in Lihue offers a fascinating glimpse into the island's past. One of the earliest Hawaiian sugar plantations, Grove Farm was founded in 1864 by George Wilcox, the son of Protestant missionary teachers at Waioli Mission in Hanalei. Planting and harvesting Grove Farm's sugar crop, which grew from 80 acres to more than 1000, ultimately involved a workforce of several hundred Hawaiians, Chinese, Koreans, Germans, Portuguese, and Filipino laborers, who brought to Kauai a rich heritage of ethnic cultures. A two-hour tour takes you through Grove Farm's cluster of buildings nestled amid tropical gardens, orchards, and rolling lawns, but be warned: the tour is extremely popular and you'll need to reserve a place at least a week in advance. You'll see the gracious old Wilcox home, the large rooms cooled by breezes from shaded verandas, and elegantly furnished with oriental carpets, magnificent koa wood floors and wainscotting, and hand crafted furniture of native woods. You will also tour the "board and batten" cottage of the plantation housekeeper, who came to Kauai, like many Japanese women, as a "picture bride" for a laborer to poor to travel home to select his wife in person. All buildings are covered by traditional "beach sand paint" (literally sand thrown against wet paint) to protect them against both heat and damp for as long as 20 years. The leisurely, friendly tour includes a stop in the kitchen for cookies and mint ice tea. For students and scholars, the library's extensive collection of Hawaiiana and plantation records is available by appointment.

Like other Hawaiian sugar plantations, Grove Farm was established at a significant point in the economic history of the islands. In the 1850's, the monarchy first began to sell land, and Hawaii entered the age of private property. Before this time, land was never sold but given in trust to subjects in pie shaped slices from the interior mountains to the sea, so that each landhold would include precious fresh water as well as coastline.

The Wilcox family, particularly two Wilcox women, made significant contributions to the development of Kauai. Elsie Wilcox, a Kauai School Commissioner, was the first woman in the territory to be elected to the Senate, and Mabel Wilcox, a public health nurse, was decorated by both France and Belgium for outstanding service during World War I. Elsie and Mabel restored Waioli Mission House in Hanalei (open T-Sat 9 am-3 pm), and Mabel planned the Grove Farm Homestead in 1971 when she was 89. Grove Farm Tours are conducted Monday, Wednesday, and Thursday at 10 am and 1:15 pm. Reserve by phone (245-3202) or by writing in advance (PO Box 1631, Lihue HI 96766). Admission.

If the Grove Farm tour doesn't fit into your schedule, you can visit the **Kauai Museum** on Rice St in downtown Lihue Monday-Friday 9:30 am-4:30 pm. The Rice Building exhibits the "Story of Kauai"—the volcanic eruptions which shaped the land, the Polynesians who voyaged to the island in canoes, the missionaries who altered its culture, and the sugar planters who, like George Wilcox, defined much of its agricultural destiny. To complement this permanent display, the monthly exhibits in the adjacent Wilcox building feature the work of local artists as well as the contributions of Kauai's different ethnic cultures. For example, one summer we saw an exhibit of Japanese, Chinese, Hawaiian, and Filipino wedding dress and traditions. Another time, we explored a marvelous retrospective on Filipinos in Kauai, from their arrival in 1906 as poorly paid laborers to present day achievements in education and social work. Once each month, the museum sponsors a free "Aloha Friday" lecture by a guest speaker. The museum shop has the most extensive collection of books on Kauai and Hawaii for sale on the island. Admission $3/adults. For information about exhibits and lectures, call 245-6931.

Halfway between Kapa'a and Princeville, be sure to visit the Kilauea Lighthouse, built in 1913, which once warned mariners away from Kauai's rugged north coast until technology replaced light flashes with radio transmissions. Come for spectacular views of the coastline and Mukuaeae island, and if you're lucky, a glimpse of Spinner Dolphins or Humpback Whales on summer vacation in the waves. This is the northernmost point of Kauai, and changes in weather are often first detected by the weather station here. Best of all, you will see a tiny part of the Hawaiian Island National Wildlife Refuge, which shelters more than 10 million seabirds in a chain of islands scattered over 1200 miles of ocean. You may see the Red-footed Booby as well as other interesting birds and plants, and hear the amazing story of how seamen carried 4 tons of French prisms up a sheer cliff to build the giant clam shaped light. Open 10 am until 4 pm weekdays ($2 admission). Call 828-1413 for tour information.

More of Kauai's rare birds and plants can be seen at the **Koke'e Natural History Museum** in Koke'e State Park. If you are interested in exploring the island's natural history, visit the museum daily between 10 am and 4 pm (335-9975). Donations welcome!

The guided tour of **Pacific Tropical Botanical Garden** in Lawai is an extraordinary opportunity to explore a 186 acre preserve of tropical fruits, spices, trees, rare plants, and flowers of astonishing variety and beauty. You can find 50 different kinds of banana and 500 species of palm. Instead of a formal garden, the plant collections are part of the natural landscape of the Lawai Valley. The tour includes a portion of the famed Lawai Kai, the Allerton family's spectacular private gardens, which have transformed this lovely valley into a rustic paradise, watered by an ingenious system of fountains, streams, waterways, and rocky pools. Wandering the shaded pathways, you will come upon a pavillion just perfect for relaxed contemplation, or a marble bench placed under a spreading, giant tree, or a statue reflecting a graceful image in a pool speckled with fallen leaves. With brilliant design and engineering, the gardens express the best of both art and nature, beautifully harmonized and balanced. Reserve your place well in advance by calling 332-8131 or writing to PO Box 340, Lawai HI 96765, as the 3-hour tour, conducted 9 am and 1 pm weekdays , or 9 am Saturdays and 1 pm Sundays, is usually fully booked and limited to the capacity of a small bus. Tickets are $10/pp, or consider a family membership ($25) which includes free tours. If some of your party do not share a horticultural interest, you might plan to drop them off at Poipu Beach Park while you visit with the flowers!

If you'd like to explore the unspoiled forests of Moloka'i, you might consider taking the short flight to this island for the tour conducted on the second Saturday of each month by the Nature Conservancy of Hawaii. The 2,274 acre Kamakou Preserve contains rare birds and 250 kinds of plants, almost all of which live nowhere else except Hawaii, as well as spectacular gorges, rain forests, bogs and sand dunes. The all-day tour costs $5 for members of the conservancy and $10 for non-members. Contact the Nature Conservancy of Hawaii, 1116 Smith St, Suite 201, Honolulu HI 96817 (808) 537-4508. Reserve at least a month in advance.

Hiking and Camping

For those who have honed their bodies into the toughness of steel, hiking can be a spectacular way to see Kauai, for more than half of the island's 551,000 square miles is forestland, and many of its most beautiful regions are inaccessible by car. However, hiking Kauai is not without risks. Many trails can become dangerous from washouts and mudslides, and in the Na Pali coastal region, where trails are often etched into the sides of sheer cliffs, hikers must be wary of waves crashing over the rocks without warning, as well as vegetation which masks the edge of a sheer drop. A good friend, for example, broke his ankle last summer when plants gave way under his feet near the edge of a ravine.

Careful planning is a must. Before your trip, write the **Division of Forestry**, Kauai District, PO Box 1671, Lihue HI 96766 for an information packet with maps and descriptions of trails (enclose $2.40 in stamps). A large selection of books and maps for hiking and camping on Kauai and other Hawaiian islands is available from **Hawaii Geographic Society**, PO Box 1698, Honolulu HI 96806.

Or write to the **Sierra Club,** PO Box 3142 Lihue HI 96766 for information and schedule of guided hikes, twice a month on Saturdays or Sundays (or call 808/946-8494). When you arrive on Kauai, call the **Division of Forestry i**n Lihue (245-4444) for a report on current trail conditions. You can also call the **Hawaii Visitor's Bureau** in Lihue (245-3971) for advice and help in arranging hiking trips, and finding local guides. One such outfit is **Local Boy Tours,** PO Box 3324, Lihue HI 96766, which will organize a hike a group of up to six, lasting anywhere from a half-day ($40/pp) to a four-day ($500/pp) expedition. Write or phone (808/822-7919) at least two weeks in advance to obtain permits.

The most famous trail, the Kalala'u, is a strenuous as well as spectacular 11 mile hike through the Na Pali cliff region. If your body is reasonably sound, you will enjoy the first few miles. This subsection, the Hanakapi'ai trail, has breathtaking views of the coast. About 1/4 mile past Ke'e Beach is a magnificent view of the beach and the Ha'ena Reefs. Bring old sneakers as the trail can be muddy, and it is not appropriate for children. Two miles of moderate up and down hiking will bring you to Hanakapi'ai Beach, nestled like a brilliant jewel in a picturesque, terraced valley. Unfortunately, this beach has currents far too dangerous for swimming, and the riptides can be so powerful that last year one unwary hiker standing in the surf at knee level was caught up in a sudden, large wave, pulled out to sea and drowned. These trails begin where paved road ends on the north coast, at Ke'e Beach, the last dependable source of drinking water. Plan on carrying your own drinking water on your hike because the bacteria leptospirosis is found in many of Kauai's rivers and streams. A good source of information about trails and conditions in the Na Pali region is **Hanale'i Camping and Backpacking** (826-6664).

The Koke'e forest region and Alakai swamp are beautiful in a different way. Within this 4,345 acre wilderness preserve are 45 miles of trails, from pleasant walks to rugged hikes, as well as fresh water fishing streams. From the Koke'e Lodge, day hikers can choose from three trails which explore the plateau and Waimea Canyon rim, ranging from the half-mile Black Pipe Trail to the 1 1/2 mile Canyon Trail along the north rim of Waimea Canyon, past upper Wa'ipo'o Falls to the Kumuwela Overlook. From this perch you can see the canyon's 3,600-foot depth and 10 mile stretch to the sea. For longer hikes, you can arrange for guides, as well as hunting and fishing licenses, at the Koke'e Lodge. The Lodge also serves meals and cocktails, and rents cabins (including refrigerator, stove, hot showers, cooking and eating utensils, linens and bedding, and even fireplaces) for only $35-$45/night for a maximum stay of 5 nights during a 30 day period. For information and reservations, write **Koke'e Lodge**, Box 819, Waimea HI 96796. (808) 335-6061. Bring warm clothes for cold nights, and remember, on Kauai as elsewhere, to lock your gear and luggage in the trunk of your car before you head for the trails.

Campers can choose from several state and county parks, for example Anahola, Ha'ena, Anini, Salt Pond, and Polihale Beach Parks. Camping is also permitted in specified areas of the Na Pali region and other wilderness preserves. For information, permits, and reservations, write the Department of Land and Natural Resources, **Division of State Parks**, P.O. Box 1671, Lihue HI 96766 or call (808) 245-4444. For information about hiking in the Alakai Swamp or hiking and camping in Waimea Canyon, contact Hawaii Division of Forestry, at the same address.

Riding and Running

The guided trail rides at **Po'oku Ranch** in Hanalei are a unique way to explore Kauai's beautiful north shore. The one hour valley ride ($15) takes you across Princeville Ranch lands, and the two hour Beach Ride ($30) takes you through fields and down to Anini Beach, first along the road, and then briefly across the sand. For the more adventurous, a three hour ride to a waterfall includes a picnic lunch and swimming ($50). Call 826-6777 for reservations.

The ride proceeds at a walk, so that inexperienced riders will have no difficulty with their means of transportation, although experienced riders may find the unvaried slow pace somewhat frustrating. The horses are well-fed and well-treated, and every effort is made to keep the ride safe and pleasurable. Tack is western unless you request an English saddle ($3 extra). While the vistas are magnificent, you could see much the same views by driving a rented car along the Anini beach road. And should it start to rain, you'd be better off under your roof! If you prefer the slow, steady pace of trail riding, however, join the early morning group to avoid the heat of the day, and wear sunglasses, or a hat which won't blow off, for once you're on board, it's hard to climb down and chase it!

Those who live to run can dream about competing in the **Pepsi Challenge** 10,000 meter run in August (P O Box 1889, Lihue HI 96766) or the **Garden Island Marathon** on Kauai's west end over Labor Day weekend (P O Box 3156, Lihue HI 96766). Request a free map of Kauai's popular running routes from the **Hawaii Council for Safe Running,** P O Box 23169, Honolulu 96822 (include stamps), or call the Council's "Runner's Hotline" (808) 245-4144 for information about running clubs and events. For a free schedule of the more than 90 races, triathalons and fun-runs state-wide, send a SASE to Tommy Kono, Dept of Parks and Recreation, City and County of Honolulu, 650 King St, Honolulu HI 96813. Remember the sun! Extra fluids and sunscreen are a must!

Hawaiian Entertainment

Hawaiian entertainment is available in different settings at a range of prices. The most expensive is the combination show and Polynesian luau, a buffet including kalua pig, sweet and sour chicken, fish, fruits, poi, salads, and the like. On different nights of the week you can try this version at the Sheraton hotels in Poipu, Kapa'a, and Princeville, the Kauai Resort Hotel and the Coco Palms or Paradise Pacifica in Wailua, or you can take an evening luau cruise with Smith's Boat tours. Some of the best shows are free! Thursday, Friday and Saturday at 4 pm, come to the Coconut Plantation Marketplace south of Kapa'a for an excellent production! Or try the Kiahuna Shopping Center on Mondays. Mosey over to the Coco Palms Hotel grounds and watch the dinner show, which starts around 9 pm, from the lawn. The shows vary nightly.

If you visit during summer months, you'll be able to enjoy another kind of festive entertainment, the bon dances held at island Buddhist temples to celebrate the ancestors of the congregation. Old and young dance together in large circles under colorful, lighted lanterns. Food, from shave ice to sushi, is usually available. At the last dance of the summer, the lanterns are set in rafts and towed out to sea near Spouting Horn. For a schedule of the dances, write to Waimea Shingon Mission, 3770A Pule Rd, Waimea HI 96796.

Golf Courses

Princeville Makai, Hanalei (826-3580), designed by Robert Trent Jones, Jr, is a 27-hole championship course with 3 challenging nines: Lake, Woods, and Ocean, famous for spectacular views and the dramatic 141-yard seventh hole, where the ocean, foaming like a cauldron, separates tee and green. The new 18-hole Prince Albert Golf Course is set in rolling pastureland. Daily fees for resort guests are $29/27 holes or $22/18 holes. Non-guests pay $52/27 holes or $38/ 18 holes. Carts are required: $13/27 holes, $9 pp.

Kiahuna Golf Course, Poipu (742-9595), designed by Robert Trent Jones, Jr. is an 18–hole links-style course, predominantly flat, with smooth, fast greens and tradewind challenges. At 6,353 yards from the tips, this course is geared more for the recreational golfer. Daily fees: $45/18 holes or $22/9 holes, including shared cart. $25 after 3 pm.

Wailua Municipal Golf Course, Wailua (245-8092). Ranked in top 25 U.S. municipal courses by *Golf Digest*, this popular 18-hole, 6658-yard course is built along the Pacific on rolling terrain amid ironwood trees and coconut palms. Fairways are narrow, greens smallish, and grass on the tough side. Fees are unbeatable: $11 on weekends or $10 on weekdays. Carts cost $11.50/18 holes or $6.75/9 holes, and pullcarts are available.

Kukuiolono Golf Course, Kalaheo (322-9151). 9-holes with spectacular views. Honor system: $5/green fees and $5/cart.

Westin Kauai, Lihue (245-5050). Designed by Jack Nicklaus, the 262–acre Kiele course is designed for golfers with a 20-handicap or better. The front nine is long and rugged with many mounds and swales. The back nine runs out to the ocean, with spectacular views of waves crashing against the rocks, and prevailing tradewinds of up to 15 mph on the southeast corner. Restricted to 120 golfers a day with tee times at 15-minute intervals, it is an extra-long course (7000 yards) with 4 tees. The Kauai Lagoons course is more accessible to the recreational golfer, a shotmaker's course with many bunkers and more undulating greens. 6,942 yards from the tips. $95 for resort guests; $125 non-guests.

Island Tastes

For a taste of Kauai's local flavor, visit the Sunshine Farmer's Markets on Wednesdays in Kapa'a at 3.00 pm, and on Fridays in Lihue at 3:30 pm, or at noon on Mondays in Koloa next to the firehouse. Come early for the best selection! From truck beds, tiny stands, or the trunks of cars, local farmers will sell their fruits, vegetables, and flowers at prices more reasonable than the super-markets. And the manoa lettuce, as low as $1.00 for a half dozen small heads, will be fresh from the garden and taste of Kauai's sunny skies and salt air. You'll never want iceberg again! You may find avocados at 3 for $1; fresh basil, oregano, marjoram, or chives; a shiny dark purple eggplant with just the right sound when you thump it. You'll see bananas of all kinds—Williams, and Bluefield, and of course, Kauai's special apple-bananas. Don't be put off by the short, fat, drab-skinned exterior, for inside the fruit is the color of golden sand at sunset and tastes of bananas laced with apples!

If you see Iris at the Kapa'a market, she may offer you a slice of her star fruit to sample, or a selection of honey sweet orange with deceptively green skin, or a slice of juicy pineapple topped with passion fruit (or call her at 822-3568). The papayas will be giants, the Waimanalo variety if you're lucky, for their red-orange center rivals the color of the sun. Try fresh limes to spark the papaya's mellow sweet flavor with tartness. Even if you aren't cooking, you'll be tempted by stringbeans as long as shoelaces, squash with squeaky skins, tomatoes still warm and fragrant, and all kinds of oriental vegetables with odd shapes. You may even find leis of pakalana or plumeria for $1 a strand! Be ready to bargain if you are buying in quantity from one seller, and take their advice about venturing into new tastes. On Wednesdays the market will be in the parking lot opposite the armory in Kapa'a. Take Kukui Road off Rt 56 and turn right at the end; then make the next right onto Kahau Road and look for the armory parking lot on your left. These days many more people are coming to Kapa'a market, and you'll find a rope tied across the parking lot which looks—and serves—as a starting line, complete with a shrill whistle, to ensure an equal chance for buyers and sellers. It drops at five minutes to 3 pm! Don't be late! On Fridays the market is held in the parking lot next to Vidinha Stadium on Kapule Hwy (Rt 51) between Ahukini Road and Rice Street. Most sellers price in $1 packages, so bring plenty of singles!

If you can't make it to the markets, stop by at Banana Joe's just north of Kilauea on Rt 56. Banana Joe makes one of the most scrumptious snacks known to man—a papaya or a banana smoothie, created by whipping up the frozen fruits until they are light as sea foam. Also try the Cuban red bananas grown right next to the fruit stand. You will be astonished at the variation in banana flavors, and you'll never look at the Chiquita label in the supermarket quite as smugly again!

Though most fresh meats are flown into Kauai from the mainland, beef raised on Kauai's sloping pastures can be bought at the supermarkets. Some island farms raise tastier beef than others, so you have to know where to go. At the N.Yoniji Store on the Corner of Rice St and Kalena St in Lihue, you can find beef raised on the Rice Ranch in Kipu near Koloa, where Mrs Rice still puts in a full day on horseback at 76. But then she's always been extraordinary. When she and her infant son were plucked from their home on Kalapaki Beach by the tsunami of 1946, she just held tight to his nightgown and kept his head above water until they were rescued! At Yoniji's store, you can catch a glimpse of Kauai before shopping centers. Browse through its remarkable assortment of furniture, clothing, and all kinds of foods! For the freshest local fish, try J & R Seafood, 4361 Rice St in Lihue (245-9946), which supplies some of the best restaurants! Rick Sato will be happy to cut you filets of whatever has just been hooked—shibiko (baby yellow fin tuna), ono, ulua, and local snappers of all hues—pink, grey, red. In summer, prices per pound start at $5, though in winter, when fish are harder to catch, prices go up to $11. Rick will create a sashimi platter, complete with sauces, especially for you! The adventurous can try opihi (limpets) raw in the shell with seaweed, or smoked marlin. In Kapa'a, try the Kuhio Market on Rt 56, one block south of the park, or Pono Fish Market on Rt 56 in Waipouli.

Kauai Specialties

If you have some extra money to spend, you won't find a more special souvenir than a Kauaian batik design by Doris Foster. Her spectacular fabrics, printed and dried in sunny Spouting Horn, can be custom stitched during your stay into a reasonably priced Aloha shirt or sundress that you will see nowhere else. You can choose from many motifs, including sand dollars, sea shells, or tropical flowers, and from brilliant colors like turquoise, royal blue, cerise, and emerald, as well as more muted shades. Doris's backless sundress is unique, and as comfortable as it is beautiful. Her newest fabric designs combine 2, even 3 colors for extraordinarily striking effects. You can see some of her fabrics at the Kapaia Stitchery or call Doris to arrange a private appointment (742-1720).

Another talented batik artist named Trish designs wonderful cotton knit shirts with tropical fish, flowers, and fruits, in all the colors of sunsets over the ocean — wonderful pinks and oranges, purples and blues, yellows and reds. Trish works with the finest, softest, lightest cotton knit fabrics that feel like a whisper next to your skin. You'll never want to wear anything else again! Trish's shirts are available at Skids at Kiahuna Shopping Village, Batik Boutique at Coconut Marketplace, and Cane Field Clothing at Kilohana, or you can order direct by mail, perhaps just in time for Christmas or a birthday. For a price list, write Designs by Trish, 319 Eggerking Rd, Kapa'a, HI 96746.

Displayed in most island galleries, pottery by Mark White and Nancy Smith of Koloa is another special, unique souvenir. Their lovely bowls, platters, and cups are glazed to capture the beautiful colors and contours of Kauai's mountains, sea, and sky. As you sip your morning coffee back home, holding one of their generous, perfectly balanced mugs in your hand, you can close your eyes and imagine the island, waiting for you, sparkling in the sun. Macadamia nut cookies taste like Kauai even if you're back home. Try several island bakeries: Kauai Kookie Kompany, sold in Big Save Markets or Tip Top Bakery in Lihue. In the Waipouli Complex, Po Po's mixes these heavenly nuts with chocolate chips or coconut into a confection Mrs Fields would envy! Kauai Soap is especially gentle and fragrant because of painstaking care and high quality standards in its production. Try coconut or plumeria!

Kukui jams and syrups are the best! Be sure to sample some heavy, coconut syrup on your pancakes and guava-strawberry jam on your PBJs. Stop in at the factory in Kalaheo and make up your own gift boxes (four 6 oz jars cost about $6). You can pack them in your suitcases, or have them shipped (postage about $3/box). Call Mr Tateishi (332-9333) to be sure the office is open. Take Rt 50 west, pass the junction with Rt 530, drive .8 mile and turn into a driveway on your right. There's no sign to mark the driveway, but you'll soon see the light blue building ahead. Don't pass up the Kukui specialty: macadamia nuts dusted with powdered chocolate! Or the new barbecue sauce. While you're in Kalaheo, try some double yolked eggs from the Madeiros chicken farm (332-8211).

If you're considering a wedding on Kauai, Kathryn Lowry can save you time, effort, and worry about the arrangements, including such special touches as horse drawn carriages and flower showers. She and her husband avoid the commercial locations, and instead help find exactly what you might be looking for—a ceremony in a private garden, on a secluded beach, or even on a yacht. They can also arrange for flowers, a photographer, and the appropriate minister. Contact Wedding in Paradise, PO Box 340, Waimea HI 96796. (808) 335-3502.

Flower Leis

The fragrance of pikake or white ginger; the cool, silky touch of petals; the delicate yet rich colors of orchids and plumeria—even in words, flower leis conjure up moonlit nights and ocean breezes. No vacation is complete without one, especially on your last night.

Many stores offer ready-made leis in a refrigerated case, but these strings of imported carnations cannot compare with a local lei which reflects the traditions of the island as well as the individual artistry of the lei maker. Order your lei a day in advance and pick it up on your way out to dinner!

At **Fujimoto's** in Lihue (245-8088), a family-owned florist carries on local traditions. The Mauna Loa lei ($15), is a wide woven band of small purple orchids; very handsome, it is often given to boys at graduation. Or try the slender strand of fragrant green Pakalana ($3/strand of 100 flowers), or another one of our favorites, the lei of white ginger, a spectacular creation of white buds so fragrant that heads will turn as you walk by. The tightly threaded ginger blossoms look almost like white feathers. Or if the blossoms are in season, try a beautiful Ilima lei made of papery orange-colored blossoms, very rare and difficult to string.

The **Coco Palms Florist** in Wailua will even deliver if you are in the local area. The small, white stephanotis, similar in shape to a lilac blossom and even more fragrant, can be threaded in single strands ($2.50) or in a thick round "triple" lei ($12) of 300 flowers, striking to look at though heavy to wear. Pikake, a tiny and delicate white flower, is the Hawaiian lei for weddings and has a wonderful, spicy scent ($4.50/strand).

Plumeria leis are the most common. Usually white or yellow and sometimes pink or deep red, the large blossoms have a wonderful perfume. A plumeria lei will last only a day, but it is relatively inexpensive, especially if you buy from Albert Christian in Anahola, who picks 7,000 blossoms each morning from his 300 trees. To visit Mr Christian, turn off Rt 56 just south of Anahola onto Kukuihale St, then turn right onto Makaio St. Follow the signs to his driveway, drive up to a gate studded with hubcaps, and obey the sign to "Honk!" Be sure to call in advance to order a single strand ($2.50) or a double ($5). You can request a lei with red, yellow and pink blossoms if you call a day ahead (822-5691).

For something out of the traditional line, stop in at **The Lei Shoppe** in Waipouli (822-1927), just across Rt 56 from McDonald's. In addition to "orchid jewelry" made with large and elegant purple, yellow, or white orchids, you'll find traditional leis with a new look. A lei of pikake and pakalana ($12.50) with a shoulder corsage of orchids is a fabulous mingling of fragrances. Some flowers last a long time with proper refrigeration, but even the fragile blossoms like pikaki and pakalana can be dried after wearing to make a wonderful tropical potpourri!

Surprisingly, you will have no trouble wearing a lei through agricultural inspection and onto the plane home, though the flowers quickly turn brown in air conditioning. Many shops will package leis for your return trip, so that they remain fresh to cheer your first morning home!

Shopping

It's hard to believe, but the best buys in the standard tourist gifts can be found at Woolworths and Long's Drugs in the **Kukui Grove Shopping Center** in Lihue. Some specialty shops on the island really are special, however, and we keep finding more. Be sure to stop at **The Kapaia Stitchery** just north of Lihue on Rt 56 (If you take the bypass road, you'll miss it!). Julie Yukimura has collected a tasteful array of women's clothes at very reasonable prices. Many items are handcrafted by island seamstresses who still make quilts and dresses with the same care their own grandmothers did. In fact, Julie's grandmother, an artist with crochet, creates absolutely beautiful vests, shawls, and dresses priced well below what work of this quality sells for on the mainland. Another woman in her '80's designs and stitches patchwork quilts, one featuring Japanese doll figures in different costumes, a great gift for a new baby. Men's Aloha shirts made by Julie's seamstresses sell for less than mass produced shirts in many stores, and you can even custom order one from Julie's wide selection of 100% cotton fabrics in beautiful Hawaiian designs. A local success story, the Stitchery is run by three generations of Kauai women — Julie, her grandmother, and Julie's delightful mother, who takes care of customers.

The Goldsmith's Gallery in the Kinipopo Shopping Village features fine jewelry crafted of gold, silver, and precious gems by five artist-craftsmen. Eric Vogt and the other award-winning design-ers will also be happy to show you albums of photographs of their designs, or to devise something special just for you, like a gold charm in the shape of a petroglyph or one of those fish you saw on the reef while snorkeling. On Rt 56 in Kapa'a, **Jim Saylor** special-izes in jewelry designs with precious stones. Lovely rings, neck-laces, and bracelets are on display, although Jim will also be happy to create something unique according to your specifications.

For coral jewelry, try **Gem** and **Linda's Creations** in Lihue, and the handful of shops in the **Coconut Plantation Marketplace** such as **The Coral Grotto** or **The Black Pearl**. Or try **Khristopher-Dion** in the new Kinipopo Shopping Center in Wailua. Cheaper prices can be found at the daily outdoor flea market at **Spouting Horn** or at the **Hawaiian Trading Post** at the junction of Rt 50 and Rt 530 near Koloa. At **Remember Kauai** or **The Shell Factory** on Rt 56 near the Coconut Plantation Marketplace in Wailua, you can have shell jewelry designed. Bring shells you find yourself, or select from the wide variety on hand in the stores. At **The Only Show in Town** in Kapa'a, you'll find an eclectic collection of inexpensive and unusual souvenirs, antiques and artifacts.

Well off the beaten track in Kilauea, **Kong Lung** offers a striking collection of antiques, souvenirs, beautiful gourmet cookware and tableware, and Hawaiian style shirts and dresses, including a special place for children. The owners have faithfully restored the

old plantation store building, constructed of lava rock, and filled it with marvelous giftware, including their own line of Hawaiian jewelry. Also in Kilauea, stop in at **Hawaiian Art Museum and Bookstore** for one of the most interesting collections of books and artifacts anywhere! In Hanalei, stop in at **Ola's** for puzzles, glass, jewelry, wooden bowls, and baskets by island and mainland artists.

The island has many unique clothing shops. **See You in China** in the Kukui Grove Center offers handpainted cotton and silk attire, unique jewelry, scarves, and handbags, and gift items. Further north in Waipouli, stop in at **Marta's Boat** for children's wear, much of it handcrafted by Marta herself. A mother who appreciates 100% cotton fabrics, Marta sells batiks and handpainted shirts by island artists in children's and women's sizes, though you will find prices on the high side. At **Nightengayles** in Kapa'a, you'll find an attractive assortment of colorful and comfortable women's clothes imported from all the islands, as well as interesting jewelry and artwork.

A hard-working Kauai family has built the **Happy Kauaian Shops** from one store to more than a dozen branches in island hotels as well as the Coconut Plantation Marketplace. Their secret to success is reasonable prices for Hawaiian-style clothing and gifts, with a particularly good selection of children's clothes.

At **Lady Jane's** in Wailua, shopping can be especially pleasant, because the proprietors, a Kauai family for generations, will offer you fragrant tea, a comfortable chair, and interesting conversation while you browse the collection of hardwoods, beautiful aloha wear, baskets, and jewelry, particularly shell jewelry made from the rare Kauai sunrise shell. Call 245-1814 to arrange free transportation to the shop from the Wailua area.

Kauai has several fine art galleries. In Koloa's **Kahana Ki'i Gallery**, you'll find a wide variety of work by Kauai's best artists— beautiful batiks, porcelains, jewelry, handpainted silk scarves, needlework, original oils, watercolors, and drawings, as well as Ron Kent's fine, almost translucent wood bowls. **Stone's Prints** in the Kukui Grove Center has a wide assortment of works by local artists. At **The Gallery at the Waiohai** in Poipu, works by artists from all over the world with a common interest in Hawaii are displayed in beautifully crafted cabinets designed and created by Terry Wells of Kauai. The blown glass and Ni'ihau shell leis are exquisite, and you'll also see pottery by Mark White and Nancy Smith. **The Gallery at Kilohana** offers photographs, acrylics, prints, woodwork and other crafts by artists from Oahu and Kauai at a wide range of prices. At the **Stones of Kilohana** on the plantation grounds, you'll find artifacts of the Pacific, including ceremonial items, baskets, and koa bowls. **Kahn Gallery** at the Coconut Plantation Marketplace features paintings with an island emphasis and fine Ni'ihau shell leis.

In Poipu's Kiahuna Shopping Village, you'll find **Elephant Walk,** which displays elegant koa furniture and frames, as well as lovely prints and ceramics. Nearby, **Tideline Gallery** and **The Ship Store Gallery** often feature exclusive showings of works by artists of national reputation. If your interests run to needlework, you can purchase kits for classic Hawaiian designs in needlepoint or crochet at **The Station** in Hanapepe (or send $2 for a catalog of 100 designs to PO Box 67, Hanapepe HI).

For the best buys in souvenir items, don't overlook department stores like Sears, Penney's, Longs, and Woolworths at Kukui Grove Center. The **Whalers General Store** in Kiahuna Shopping Center and Coconut Plantation Marketplace often advertises specials on taste treats like macadamia nuts and coffee. If you're looking for the perfect T-shirt, try **Crazy Shirts**, whose shirts resist fading and shrinking. Wash them inside out. One of our favorite family stops is **M. Miura Store** in Kapa'a, an old-time local business where you can pick out souvenir T-shirts from a huge assortment at affordable prices, plus shorts, beachwear, mu mus and aloha shirts, and even boogie boards! Service is very friendly and the store uncrowded. If you need help with your camera, **Don's Camera Center** on Rice St in Lihue can give you quick, efficient, professional advice. You can also rent cameras and have your film developed quickly.

Remember: Now that Kauai has entered the modern world, the Seven/Eleven accepts Visa and Master Card, and Foodland is open 24 hours!

Children's Corner

The free hula show Thursday, Friday, and Saturday afternoons at 4 pm at the Coconut Plantation Marketplace in Kapa'a is a favorite with our children year after year. The show is great, with lots of music and dancing, and the kids don't have to sit in one place but can walk or run around and even climb some of the structures made from sugar mill machinery. While the kids enjoy the show, adults can browse the many shops.

Several beaches offer playground areas for children (Hanama'ulu, Poipu Beach Park), one offers lifeguard protection (Poipu Beach Park), and a few offer protected swimming areas for small children (Poipu Beach Park, Lydgate State Park). Fishing with nets is fun at the rivers behind the beaches at Anahola and Moloa'a, and at the tidal pools at Salt Pond Beach Park and Poipu Beach Park. If you bring some stale bread, the fish will swim right up to you. With this bait, kids can have lots of fun snorkeling even in very shallow water. The best spot for family snorkeling is Lydgate Park, where fish are trapped in the lava-ringed pools. For all around family fun in summertime, when the surf on the northern shore is gentle enough, our favorite beach is at Kalihiwai Bay, where you can wade and fish in the river, boogie board in the waves, and the sand is perfect for castles. In winter time, try Lydgate Park, or on the south shore, Salt Pond Beach Park and Poipu Beach Park. At any time, should you spot any small blue jellyfish on the sand, go to another beach for the day; these Portuguese men 'o war, which sometimes wash ashore after a storm, really sting!

A small zoo behind the Coco Palms Hotel in Wailua is a popular spot for children. Any coconuts they can find among the palm trees are theirs to keep! Adults can husk and crack the coconuts open right there by using a stake positioned in the ground for that purpose. Adults will enjoy reading the names of famous persons who have dedicated individual coconut palms in the grove. At 7:30 each evening, torches in the grove are lit by Hawaiians in costume who recreate an ancient ceremony. Kids love the spectacle and don't seem to mind the black smoke! No admission charge.

The Westin is a children's wonderland. Kids will love a visit to the stable where Fergie, all of 19 hands high, loves a pat, and they will also enjoy a carriage ride through the hotel grounds. Throughout the hotel, the staff is pleasant and particularly accommodating to children, who will love the enormous pool, complete with bridge to the island in the center, and the five jaccuzzis. The hotel will take a whole morning to explore!

If children collect shells and sand during visits to the beach, they can have fun with art projects on rainy days back home. Sand can be sprinkled over glue in all sorts of designs for "sand paintings". Kids will also enjoy gluing small shells to small plastic or cardboard boxes to give as gifts. Small shells can be glued onto pieces of driftwood or larger shells, or even made into necklaces. In this way, children can give gifts made from their own special treasures to friends and relatives.

With a plastic pail and an inexpensive net ($4 for an 8" net at Big Save), children can have lots of fun trying to catch fish trapped in tidal pools. Nets are also great for evening "toad hunting" expeditions. Toads are plentiful on Kauai, hiding under bushes by day but hopping about after dusk just slowly enough for youngsters to occasionally net one. The fun is in the chase! Toad hunters should wear long pants and use 6-12, for mosquitoes come out at the same time the toads do!

Small tennis buffs can get some special practice with Meg Minton, who teaches tennis and swimming at the Sheraton Coconut Beach Hotel. Tennis and Swim Summer Camp meets 2 mornings a week for 3 week sessions (the first session begins in early June). Your child may register for single days, if there is space, or for private lessons. Call Meg at 822-3455, or write in advance (PO Box 830, Kapa'a HI 96746). To our kids, Meg is a favorite teacher, and tennis camp is "Ex!" During summer months and at Christmas, special daytime camp activites are offered for children of guests at the Westin, the Waiohai, and the Sheraton Poipu Beach Hotels.

Kauai's public library system is very friendly. You can join local families for free puppet shows and talks, and even apply for a library card. For rainy days, rent a VCR and some movies. Cheapest rate is at Foodland ($2.99 for first tape; $1.49 for second) and selection of kidvid is pretty good.

Travel Tips

If you are traveling with babies or toddlers, be sure to request "extra leg-room" seating well in advance of your trip—at the time you make your reservations or, at the very latest, two weeks before departure, and double-check to be sure your seat assignments are in the airline's computer before you leave. Getting your boarding passes in advance has another, very important advantage: your seats have priority if the flight is overbooked. Don't forget to enroll in the airline's "Frequent Flyer Plan." Bonus awards include free tickets, and even if it takes years for you to accumulate the required mileage, patience and persistence just might pay off! Enroll the children too! Be sure to bring along your child's car seat, which goes into the baggage compartment with your luggage, as Hawaii state law requires them for children under three.

Airline regulations require a minimum 70 minute layover in Honolulu to allow passengers and baggage to be transferred to inter-island connecting flights on Hawaiian or Aloha Airlines. However, there is a way to beat the system and minimize time wasted in the airport. After landing in Honolulu, proceed directly to the Aloha Airlines Terminal, a ten-minute walk or $.50 bus ride. Check the departure schedule for an earlier flight, go to the ticket counter and see if you can get on, even as a stand-by if necessary (the computer data is often wrong, and stand-bys can usually get on). Changing your ticket from one carrier to the other can be done in a moment at the ticket counter. It used to be easy, when the terminals were side by side, to check schedules for both Hawaiian and Aloha Airlines at the same time, but airport renovation has separated them, and you must walk another ten minutes to check departures on Hawaiian Airlines. (Or let your fingers do the walking, and phone!) If you are able to change your flight, your luggage will remain on your originally scheduled flight, but you will be in Lihue with a head start, which you can use for filling out the forms on your rental car. Then you can drop someone off at the grocery store or leave the family at McDonald's while you go back for the baggage. On long travel days, especially with young children, this saved time can be a lifesaver!

Families who fly to Kauai from the east coast might consider staying overnight in California to help children make the difficult time adjustment in stages, particularly on the return home. After the long flight from Kauai to California, the kids can run around in the hotel, have some ice cream, and stay up as late as possible in order to push their body clocks ahead three hours while they sleep. If you can take a late morning flight out of California the next day, the kids can sleep late in the morning, and if you're lucky, they will wake up fresh for the second day's flight and be ready to adjust their body clocks another three hours. Traveling through two time zones is no snap, but this plan can make it a bit easier.

On that journey home, bad weather might delay your connecting flight from Lihue to Honolulu, and so you might consider taking a flight earlier in the day, before the inter-island flights get backed up. If you arrive in Honolulu so early that you can't hang around the airport, consider taking a cab to a Waikiki Beach hotel for brunch. The cab will cost about $13, and this plan is well worth it, for, if you are traveling with children, the consequences of missing your flight to the mainland are too awful to consider! If you have more than five in your party, you can travel in luxury in a limo for no extra charge! Brunch at the Hilton Hawaiian Village, for example, can be fun!

To amuse little ones during the long flight, pack lots of small toys, crayons, dot-to-dot books, paper dolls and scissors and an "airplane present" that can only be unwrapped when the seatbelt sign goes off! Ask the cabin attendants for "kiddie packs" or cards right away as supplies are often limited. Pack a secret snack or toy for those awful moments when one child spills coke on another! Keep chewing gum handy to help children relieve the ear-clogging which can be so uncomfortable, even painful, during the last twenty minutes of the descent when cabin pressure changes. Sucking on a bottle will help a baby or toddler

To save shopping time, we bring as many beach and swimming toys as we can fit. "Swimmies" (arm floats) are great for small children to use in the pool. Small trucks for sand-dozing, frisbees, inflatable beach balls, and floats can be stuffed into suitcase corners! Boogie boards, by far the best swimming toy, are expensive, but can be brought home in the baggage compartment after your vacation (packed in a pillowcase!). We found the best prices at Gem in Lihue, the M. Miura store in Kapa'a, and Progressive

Expressions in Koloa, which also handcrafts surfboards and skim boards. Boogie boards are better balanced than the cheaper imitations, and even small children enjoy trying to ride them. Caution: they can be hazardous in a pool; a small child who tips over in deep water can be trapped underneath.

When two suitcases disappeared during our flight home in 1982, we learned some lessons the hard way about packing. Now we pack a change of clothes, bathing suit, and toilet articles for each family member, as well as any prescription drugs, in a carry-on bag just in case someone's suitcase is lost temporarily. We also distribute everybody's belongings in every suitcase, so that no one person is left without clothes if a suitcase is lost permanently. And we label each bag clearly inside where the label can't be accidentally detached. Since one of our missing suitcases contained all our exposed film, a heartbreaking loss, we now use mailers and send each roll to Kodak immediately after removing it from the camera! Incredibly, lightning struck twice, and two more suitcases disappeared three years ago. Replacement-cost property insurance on our Homeowner's insurance policy has certainly turned out to be a wise investment, for the airline's insurance limit is $1,250 per passenger, unless you purchase increased protection at the ticket counter before the flight (usually $1 per $100). Airlines typically subtract 10% of the purchase price for each year you have owned an item, and reimbursement can take up to six months.

If your luggage is missing or damaged, be sure to save all baggage-claim stubs, boarding passes, and tickets, and be sure to fill out an official claim form at the baggage supervisor's office *before* you leave the airport. Most clearly tagged luggage makes its way to the owner within 24 hours, but if your luggage is orphaned for longer and you are out of town, most airlines will provide emergency funds of $25 a day for toiletries if you present receipts. Call the airline daily for an update on your missing bags!

Tired of hotels? For information about private homes on Kauai that take paying guests, contact Bed and Breakfast Hawaii, PO Box 449, Kapa'a HI 96746 (808/822-7771). A membership fee and list of 125 available homes is $11.

While driving your rental car on Kauai, keep this in mind: speed limits are strictly enforced, especially in residential and business areas, and so is the seat belt law. It's illegal to make a U-turn in a "business district," even if it doesn't look like much of a business district. There's not much crime on this island, so you can guess how the police occupy their time!

Suggestions from our Readers

The Dawsons of Los Angeles suggest a visit to the Waioli Mission House and Church in Hanalei. Sunday services are conducted in Hawaiian as well as English, and the very friendly family atmosphere is evident in the announcement at the top of the Sunday Bulletin:"Our *keikis* are apt to wander during church. They do this because they feel at home in God's house. Please love them as we do." Call 826-6253 for information.

The Patlers of Mill Valley, CA share their "special afternoon with Daddy": walking the beach at Hanalei Bay, crossing over to the Waioli Mission grounds to swing and shoot baskets, and ending up at the Wishing Well Gallery across from Ching Young Village for the best shave ice! Macadamia nut ice cream over shave ice is a favorite, as is lilikoi.

Polihale Beach on a very rainy day is not a good idea, according to the Franks of Edgewood, Kentucky. "We mired our car in the muddy cane road and were lucky to be pushed out by some plucky Wyoming tourists!" This advice is true of all Kauaian dirt roads

About Secret Beach, Donna Madden of Orinda, California writes, "Either you kept a secret from us or the beach kept its secret from you, because it is sometimes a nude beach...We were surprised when we got to the bottom of the path and ran into a man with long blond hair wearing nothing but a guitar." Each to his own music!

Restaurant Index

Order Form

Please send _____ copies of the
Tenth Anniversary Kauai Guide to:

I enclose $5.95 plus $2 shipping and handling.

Papaloa Press

362 Selby Lane
Atherton CA 94025